| 中国思想文化术语多语种对外翻译
标准化建设项目成果
CHINESE THINKING AND CULTURE
MULTILINGUAL TERMINOLOGY DATABASE

中华源·河南故事
CHINESE CIVILIZATION
Stories from Henan

航空城
ZHENGZHOU—AN AVIATION CITY

河南省人民政府外事办公室　编

河南大学出版社
HENAN UNIVERSITY PRESS
·郑州·

图书在版编目（CIP）数据

中华源·河南故事. 航空城：汉英对照 / 河南省人民政府外事办公室编. -- 郑州：河南大学出版社，2021.4

ISBN 978-7-5649-4610-4

Ⅰ. ①中… Ⅱ. ①河… Ⅲ. ①地方文化－河南－通俗读物－汉、英②航空运输业－河南－通俗读物－汉、英 Ⅳ. ① G127.61-49 ② F562.861

中国版本图书馆 CIP 数据核字（2021）第 062941 号

责任编辑	郑华峰			
责任校对	刘利晓			
封面设计	翟淼淼			
出版发行	河南大学出版社			
	地址：郑州市郑东新区商务外环中华大厦2401号　邮编：450046			
	电话：0371-86059701（营销部）			
	0371-86059750（高等教育与职业教育分公司）			
	网址：hupress.henu.edu.cn			
排　版	河南大学出版社设计排版部			
印　刷	河南博雅彩印有限公司			
版　次	2021年4月第1版	印　次	2021年4月第1次印刷	
开　本	710 mm×1010 mm　1/16	印　张	11	
字　数	176千	定　价	56.00元	

版权所有，侵权必究

本书如有印装质量问题，请与河南大学出版社营销部联系调换。

"中华源·河南故事"系列丛书编委会

顾　　问　黄友义　杨　平　范大祺
名誉主任　穆为民　何金平　刘炯天
主　　任　付　静
副 主 任　陈　岩　陈志伟　刁玉华　方启雄　介晓磊
　　　　　孔留安　李冰冰　李向前　李　镇　梁留科
　　　　　刘金锋　牛卫国　屈鹏飞　史永庆　田　凯
　　　　　万正峰　王建修　王清义　王自文　许二平
　　　　　杨建伟　杨玮斌　张改平　张俊峰　张明超
　　　　　张松文　赵卫东

主　　编　付　静
副 主 编　李冰冰
编　　委　陈　玮　丁　锐　高　阳　徐恒振　郑延保

中华源·河南故事·航空城

主　　编　张俊峰
副 主 编　王　飞　郭银玲（英文）
中文撰稿　杨晓峰　邓　骅　金艳阳　杨　柳
英文译者　许　峰　史春柳　王中心　李　静
英文审校　〔美国〕Nathan Suchomel

The Editorial Committee
Chinese Civilization
Stories from Henan

Consultants	Huang Youyi Yang Ping Fan Daqi
Honorary Directors	Mu Weimin He Jinping Liu Jiongtian
Director	Fu Jing
Deputy Directors	Chen Yan Chen Zhiwei Diao Yuhua Fang Qixiong
	Jie Xiaolei Kong Liu'an Li Bingbing Li Xiangqian
	Li Zhen Liang Liuke Liu Jinfeng Niu Weiguo
	Qu Pengfei Shi Yongqing Tian Kai Wan Zhengfeng
	Wang Jianxiu Wang Qingyi Wang Ziwen Xu Erping
	Yang Jianwei Yang Weibin Zhang Gaiping
	Zhang Junfeng Zhang Mingchao Zhang Songwen
	Zhao Weidong
Chief Editor	Fu Jing
Deputy Chief Editor	Li Bingbing
Editors	Chen Wei Ding Rui Gao Yang Xu Hengzhen
	Zheng Yanbao

Chinese Civilization
Stories from Henan
Aviation City

Editor-in-Chief	Zhang Junfeng
Associate Editors-in-Chief	Wang Fei Guo Yinling (English Text)
Writers	Yang Xiaofeng Deng Hua Jin Yanyang Yang Liu
Translators	Xu Feng Shi Chunliu Wang Zhongxin Li Jing
Translation Proofreaders	Nathan Suchomel (U.S.)

总　序

中国是世界四大文明古国之一，也是世界上唯一的古代文明传统未曾中断的国家。河南省地处中国中东部，是中华文明和中华民族的重要发祥地，在中国五千年的文明史上，河南作为国家政治、经济、文化的中心就长达三千多年。从某种意义上讲，一部河南史就是半部中国史。这里是中华人文始祖黄帝的故乡，是古丝绸之路的东方起点，是少林功夫和陈氏太极的发源地，这里创建了中国历史上最早的都城，镌刻了中国最古老的文字，诞生了中国最初的商业文明。

伴随着新时代的荣光，河南经济社会发展迅速，人民生活水平显著提升，这是河南人民自力更生、艰苦奋斗的历史结果，也是对外开放带来的益处。河南经济社会的发展、人民生活方式的改变都植根于深层次的文化积淀。为了让世界更多地了解河南，让河南更好地走向世界，2018年以来，河南省人民政府外事办公室认真研析了这片古老土地上的历史文化资源和时代风貌，组织各领域权威专家学者，编译了"中华源·河南故事"中外文系列丛书，选取黄河文化、河洛文化、老子、庄子、黄帝、少林功夫、太极拳、中医、汉字、丝绸之路、古都、农业、大运河、文物、陶瓷、青铜器、手工艺、书法、杂技、豫菜、豫剧、脱贫攻坚、空中丝绸之路、航空城、南水北调、中国粮谷、红旗渠、焦裕禄等多个主题，力图以故事的方式向世界展现一个立体、全面、真实的河南。

当今世界，人类文明无论是在物质还是在精神方面都取得了巨大进步，特别是物质的极大丰富，这在古代世界是完全不能想象的。同时，当代人类也面临着许多突出的难题，比如，贫富差距持续扩大，物欲追求奢华无度，个人主义恶性膨胀，社会诚信不断消减，伦理道德每况愈下，人与自然关系日趋紧张，等等。要解决这些难题，不仅需要运用人类今天的智慧和力量，而且需要运用人类历史上积累和储存的智慧和力量。河南历史文化底蕴深厚、包容性强，在今天仍极具现实意义。中原文化蕴含的思想智慧有助于修身养性，推动人类社会进步发展，焦裕禄精神、红旗渠精神所体现的为民爱民、艰苦奋斗的价值取向是构建人类命运共同体的力量源泉。我们期待与读者们一起从河南故事中汲取更多的智慧和力量，共同创造更加美好的未来。

Series Foreword

China is one of the four ancient civilizations in the world, and is also the only country in the world where the ancient civilization has not been interrupted. Located in east-central China, Henan Province is an important cradle for the Chinese nation and Chinese civilization. In the course of the five thousand years of Chinese history, for more than three thousand years it served as the political, economic and cultural center of the country and therefore, as generally accepted, represents half of the history of China. Henan is the native place of Yellow Emperor, the cradle of Chinese culture, the starting point of the ancient Silk Road in the east, and the birthplace of Shaolin Kungfu and Chen-style Taijiquan—typical examples of the world-renowned Chinese martial arts. It was here that the earliest capital city in China was founded, the oldest Chinese characters engraved, and the earliest commerce took shape.

In the new era, Henan has witnessed rapid growth in its economy and remarkable improvement of people's living conditions owing to the national reform and opening-up policy and unremitting endeavors of the people. Modern economic achievements and social development as well as the changes of way of life could be traced back to its traditional values and cultural heritages. To enable people from other countries to understand Henan, and let the Province integrate more efficiently into the world development, the Foreign Affairs Office of the People's Government of Henan Province has organized teams of authoritative experts and scholars in relevant fields to compile this *Chinese Civilization: Stories from Henan* in Chinese and foreign languages since 2018 by crystallizing the excellence of traditions and outstanding features of modern development. The book series include *The Yellow River Culture*, *Heluo Culture*, *Laozi*, *Zhuangzi*, *The Yellow Emperor*, *Shaolin Kungfu*, *Taijiquan*, *Traditional Chinese Medicine*,

Chinese Characters, *The Silk Road*, *Ancient Chinese Capitals*, *Feeding the People—Agriculture*, *The Grand Canal*, *Cultural Heritage*, *Ceramic*, *Bronze*, *Handicraft Art*, *Calligraphy*, *Acrobatics*, *Henan Cuisine*, *Henan Opera*, *Poverty Alleviation*, *Silk Road in the Air*, *Zhengzhou—An Aviation City*, *South-to-North Water Diversion*, *China Grain Valley*, *Man-Made River—Hongqiqu Canal*, *A Model Official—Jiao Yulu*, etc., presenting a panoramic picture of the Province.

In today's world, human civilization has made great progress in both material accumulation and ethical advancement, and the great abundance of materials today, especially, is beyond the imagination of the ancient people. At the same time, however, modern people are also confronted with a lot of problems, such as the widening gap between the rich and the poor, the indulgence in pursuit of luxury and extravagance, the undesirable extension of individualism, the decline of social integrity, and the increasingly tense relationship between man and nature. To solve the problems, we need to draw on the wisdom and powers developed today as well as those accumulated in the past. Henan is endowed with rich historical and cultural heritages characterized by its inclusiveness, and such heritages remain significant today. The intelligence and wisdom in Henan culture are conducive to self-cultivation and to the promotion of social development. The spirit of serving the people and relentless struggle, as embodied in Jiao Yulu and Man-Made River—Hongqiqu Canal provides source of strength for building a community with a shared future for mankind. It is our hope that wisdom and strength from Henan stories could lead us to a shared brilliant future.

前　言

郑州，地处中原要冲，历史上曾五次为都、八代为州，是华夏文明的重要发祥地之一。约5000年前，中华人文始祖轩辕黄帝建都轩辕丘，在这里肇造了中华文明；约3600年前，商汤定都于此，"三商"（商族人、商朝、商业）文化基因从此融入中原大地，声名显赫的"商都"由此而生；2000多年前，中原使者出使西域，从此，筚路蓝缕的商人，在串串驼铃声中开辟了一条连接亚欧的古丝绸之路。从原始部落到聚落城池，从城邦国家到文明王朝，历史发展的链条在此从未断裂。

时代更迭，荣光延续。如今的郑州航空港经济综合实验区，循着陆上丝绸之路的足迹，闯出了一条"靠蓝天开放"的快速发展之路，打开了郑州、河南乃至中部地区同全国各地和世界各国友好交往的窗口。

2017年6月14日，国家主席习近平在北京会见卢森堡首相格扎维埃·贝泰尔时明确表示，支持建设郑州—卢森堡"空中丝绸之路"，为航空港实验区深度融入"一带一路"建设指明了方向。

国务院总理李克强也曾分别于2015年9月和2017年5月两次到航空港实验区考察，他表示，河南承东启西、连南接北，航空港实验区、跨境电子商务实实在在地显示着中原腹地的重要力量。

2018年11月27日，河南省委书记王国生到航空港实验区调研，强调要以习近平新时代中国特色社会主义思想为指导，推动航空港实验区在高质量轨道上健康发展，让这张名片更加亮丽。

"这个事一定要当'1号工程'来做，河南的将来要靠机场。"2008年，时任河南省人民政府省长郭庚茂到河南履新不久，就把航空港实验区建设作为他第一次调研的课题。

历经数届决策者不遗余力的"接力"，2013年3月7日，《郑州航空港经济综合实验区发展规划(2013—2025年)》获国务院批复，明确其战略定位是"打造成为国际航空物流中心、以航空经济为引领的现代产业基地、内陆地区对外开放重要门户、现代航空都市和中原经济区核心增长极"。

同年4月3日，航空港实验区获批27天后，时任河南省人民政府省长谢伏瞻，在国务院新闻办公室新闻发布厅做起了河南对外的"宣传大使"，用简练、理性的语言，畅谈航空港实验区的建设思路。

由此，航空港实验区成为河南决策者们撬动经济腾飞的"支点"。一场波澜壮阔的大变革，正在改写和颠覆这片区域的发展轨迹，揭开新发展的序幕。

2020年1月2日，河南省委常委、郑州市委书记徐立毅到航空港实验区调研时强调，建设航空港实验区，是党和国家赋予郑州先行先试、探索内陆地区开放路子的重大任务，要充分发挥自身主动性，紧扣"南动"功能布局，站位全国全省发展大局，努力打造内陆地区对外开放的新优势。

在国家、省、市的正确领导与大力支持下，航空港实验区深入学习贯彻习近平总书记关于河南、郑州的要求和指示精神，落实省委、市委决策部署，保持战略定力，坚定发展信心，围绕中心、服务大局，着力打造对外开放高地。

从蹒跚学步到风华正茂，航空港实验区一路追梦高歌猛进，一路跨越势不可当。深入"一带一路"建设，开放龙头高昂，发展动力澎湃，以大枢纽带动大物流，以大产业塑造大都市。

"陆空对接、多式联运、内捷外畅"的综合交通体系，国际航空运输网、"米"字形高铁网和轨道交通网"三网"融合，中国速度"连天接地、通达全球"，河南与世界的"距离"从未如此之近。

"空中丝绸之路"正把"新鲜全球"带到中原百姓的身边，与此同时，河南的特色产品、高端制造业和高附加值农副产品等"中国制造"也通过这样一条"脉络"打入世界市场，口岸经济在航空港实验区蓬勃发展、风生水起。

瞄准智能终端、生物医药、新能源、商贸会展等系列朝阳产业，走出一条科技、绿色、健康的现代临空经济发展道路……不断释放的"溢出效应"，正带动整个河南加速融入全球产业链条，引领中部、服务全国、连通欧亚、辐射全球。

从无到有、从有到优，一个支撑航空大都市加快发展的现代产业体系正在快速构建，一座连通全球、生态宜居、智慧创新的现代化国际航空大都市正以崭新的面貌崛起于中原大地。

Preface

Zhengzhou, located at the crossroads of the Central Plains, has been the capital of China five times and served as the state for eight dynasties, and is one of the important birthplaces of Chinese civilization. About 5,000 years ago, Yellow Emperor, the ancestor of Chinese people, set his national capital at Xuanyuan Hill, where Chinese civilization was created. About 3,600 years ago, King Tang of the Shang Dynasty (about 1600 BCE - 1046 BCE) established his dynasty's capital here, the cultural gene of the "Three Shangs" (Shang people, Shang Dynasty and Shang commerce) was integrated into the Central Plains, and the famous "Shangdu" (Capital of the Shang Dynasty) was born. More than 2,000 years ago, envoys from the Central Plains were sent to the Western Regions. After that initial expedition, business people with camels loaded with goods, endured great hardships to open up the Ancient Silk Road connecting Asia and Europe. From primitive tribes to settlement cities, from city-states to civilized dynasties, the chain of historical development has never been broken here.

Times change but glory continues. Today's Zhengzhou Airport Economy Zone, following the footsteps of the Silk Road, has created a rapid development path by the "Air Silk Road" and has opened a window for friendly exchanges between Zhengzhou, Henan and the Central Plains and even all parts of the country and other countries in the world.

On June 14, 2017, when President Xi Jinping met with Xavier Bettel, Prime Minister of Luxembourg, in Beijing, he made it clear that he supported the construction of the Zhengzhou-Luxembourg "Air Silk Road" and laid out the direction for the deep integration of the Zhengzhou Airport Economy Zone into the Belt and Road Initiative.

Premier Li Keqiang of the State Council also visited the Zhengzhou Airport Economy Zone twice in September 2015 and May 2017 respectively. He said that

Henan province connects the east with the west and the south with the north. He also said that the Zhengzhou Airport Economy Zone and its cross-border e-commerce show the important strength of the hinterland of the Central Plains.

On November 27, 2018, Wang Guosheng, Secretary of the Henan Provincial Party Committee, went on an inspection tour of the Zhengzhou Airport Economy Zone, and stressed that under the guidance of Xi Jinping Thought on Socialism with Chinese Characteristics for a New Era, Zhengzhou Airport Economy Zone is supposed to attain a high and harmonious development and play an increasingly important part in the economic development of Henan province.

"This matter must be done as the 'No.1 Project', and the future of Henan depends on Zhengzhou airport," said Guo Gengmao, then Governor of the Henan Provincial People's Government. In 2008, when Guo Gengmao took up his new post in Henan, he took the construction of the Zhengzhou Airport Economy Zone as his first research topic.

After effort by successive policy makers, *The Development Planning of the Zhengzhou Airport Economy Zone (2013-2025)* was approved by the State Council on March 7, 2013, making it clear that the zone's strategic position is "an international aviation logistics center, a modern industrial base led by the aviation economy, an improtant gateway to the outside world in the inland area, a modern aviation city, and a core growth pole of the Central Plains Economy Zone".

On April 3, 2013, 27 days after the approval of the Zhengzhou Airport Economy Zone, Xie Fuzhan, then Governor of the Henan Provincial People's Government, became Henan's "propaganda ambassador" to the outside world in the press conference hall of the Information Office of the State Council. He talked about the construction plan of the Zhengzhou Airport Economy Zone in concise and rational language.

As a result, the Zhengzhou Airport Economy Zone has become the "fulcrum" for Henan policy makers to promote economic development. A magnificent change is rewriting the development track of this region and initiating new development.

On January 2, 2020, Xu Liyi, member of the Standing Committee of the Henan Provincial Party Committee and Secretary of the Zhengzhou Municipal

Party Committee, stressed during his visit to the Zhengzhou Airport Economy Zone that the construction of the Zhengzhou Airport Economy Zone is an important task entrusted by the CPC and the government to Zhengzhou to explore ways to open up inland areas. It is necessary to give full play to this initiative, stick to the functional layout of a "Vibrating South Zhengzhou", bear in mind the overall development situation of the whole province, and strive to create new opportunities for inland areas to open up to the outside world.

With the correct leadership and the strong support of the state, the province and the city, the Zhengzhou Airport Economy Zone has thoroughly studied and implemented the guiding spirit of General Secretary Xi Jinping's request on Henan and Zhengzhou, has implemented the decision-making arrangements of the Provincial Party Committee and the Municipal Party Committee, has maintained strategic determination, has strengthened development confidence, has served the overall situation, and has made great efforts to build a hub for opening up to the outside world.

All through the way, the Zhengzhou Airport Economy Zone has been chasing dreams and making great strides, and it has been unstoppable all the way. By continuing to open up to the world and by deeply integrating with the Belt and Road Initiative, the Zhengzhou Airport Economy Zone has built strong momentum, spurring the development of big logistics with the construction of a transportation hub, and shaping the metropolis with the development of industries.

The "distance" between Henan and the world has never been so short thanks to the comprehensive transportation system featuring "seamless connection between air service and road transport, multimodal transport, convenient and unimpeded transport", the integration of the international air transport network, the star-shaped high-speed rail network and the rail transit network, and China speed in all walks of life.

The "Air Silk Road" is bringing fresh food and drinks from home and abroad to the people of the Central Plains. At the same time, products "Made in China" such as Henan's specialities and traditional products, high-end manufacturing products and high value-added agricultural by-products, have also entered the world market through the "vein of the Air Silk Road". The port economy is booming and thriving in the Zhengzhou Airport Economy Zone.

Aiming at a series of emerging and cutting edge industries such as intelligent terminals, biomedicine, new energy, trade and exhibition, the Zhengzhou Airport Economy Zone has been at the forefront of a scientific, green and healthy modern airport economic development path. The continuously released "spillover effect" are driving Henan to accelerate its integration into the global industrial chain, leading the central region, serving the whole country, connecting Asia, Europe and the whole world.

From the drawing board to excellence, a modern industrial system supporting the accelerated development of an aviation metropolis is being rapidly constructed, and a modern international aviation metropolis with global connectivity, ecological habitability and intelligent innovation is rising in the Central Plains.

目 录　　　　　　　　　　　　　　　Contents

第一章　交通大枢纽　　　　　　　　　　　　001
　　一、中原开放向蓝天　　　　　　　　　　002
　　二、"贴地飞行"通八方　　　　　　　　020
　　三、连天接地"零距离"　　　　　　　　032

Chapter 1　Major Transportation Hubs　　　001
　　Ⅰ. The Central Plains Opening-up via Aviation　　003
　　Ⅱ. Flying High-speed Trains to All Directions　　021
　　Ⅲ. Zero Distance Transfer Between Air and Rail Transportation　　033

第二章　开放大门户　　　　　　　　　　　　043
　　一、口岸经济通世界　　　　　　　　　　044
　　二、一颗种子结硕果　　　　　　　　　　060
　　三、产业腾飞画蓝图　　　　　　　　　　082

Chapter 2　Opening-up to the World　　　　043
　　Ⅰ. Port Economy Connecting with the World　　045
　　Ⅱ. From Seed to Fruits　　061
　　Ⅲ. A Blueprint for Industrial Take-off　　083

第三章　航空大都市　　　　　　　　　　　　101
　　一、"飞"出一座大都市　　　　　　　　102
　　二、宜居宜业新高地　　　　　　　　　　112
　　三、智通空港引未来　　　　　　　　　　140

Chapter 3 Aviation Metropolis   101
    Ⅰ. A Metropolis Rising on Plane Wings   103
    Ⅱ. A New Destination That Is Habitable and Business-friendly   113
    Ⅲ. A Smart Airport Embraces the Future   141

结　语   152
Conclusion   153

第一章
交通大枢纽

Chapter 1

Major Transportation Hubs

一个地方的交通地位决定其战略地位，进而影响这个地方的兴衰。河南，黄帝故里，中华文化的发源地，地处中原，古时乃兵家必争之地。一百年前的这片土地上，火车拉来了郑州这座城市；一百年后的今天，当郑州与航空邂逅，依托独特的地理和交通优势，郑州航空港经济综合实验区（简称"航空港实验区"）上升为国家战略，以此为推动，将航空港实验区乃至河南省打造为全球物流版图上的"天地之中"指日可待。

　　不靠海、不沿边，内陆开放要靠"丝路"和蓝天。深处中国内陆中原腹地的航空港实验区，几年前还只是一座名不见经传的小镇，绝大多数人只知道这里有座郑州新郑国际机场（简称"新郑国际机场"）。如今，这里闯出了一条"靠蓝天开放"的快速发展之路，在航空港实验区的土地上，人们可以方便地借助飞机、高铁、地铁、高速公路等多种交通方式去往想去的任何地方……人畅其行，物畅其流，这里的繁荣与便捷让人仿佛置身于一座港口城市。

一、中原开放向蓝天

　　夜幕降临，新郑国际机场3600米跑道上，助航灯光如繁星点点，在巨大的轰鸣声中，不断有飞机滑行、起飞，心跳仿佛与天地间的震颤同频，眼前的机场早已成为"不夜城"。

　　机场是一个城市的门户，在一定程度上代表着一个城市乃至整个地区的发展水平。20多年前，一座崭新的机场——新郑国际机场顺利建成通航。身处内陆的中原，从此有了蓝天的高度。20多年来，机场跑道拉近了郑州与世界的距离，方便了中原百姓的出行。

　　郑东新区CBD，高楼林立，车流如织，已然成为展示郑州城市建设，乃至河南的一个亮点和窗口。然而在20世纪50年代，这片区域还是连绵起伏的沙丘，郑州最早的机场——郑州燕庄机场（简称"燕庄机场"），就曾建在这里。

The transportation status of a place determines its strategic position, which affects the rise and fall of this place. Henan, the hometown of Yellow Emperor and the birthplace of Chinese culture, is located in central China and was a battleground for military strategists in ancient times. A hundred years ago, trains boosted the development of Zhengzhou; today when Zhengzhou is fueled by aviation, relying on its unique geographical and transportation advantages, the Zhengzhou Airport Economy Zone has been elevated to a national strategy. Thus, it is just around the corner to build the zone and even Henan as the global logistics hub of air and land transportation.

Not alongside the sea or the border, the inland depends on the Silk Road and aviation to open. Located in the hinterland of China's Central Plains, the Zhengzhou Airport Economy Zone was only a little-known town a few years ago when the vast majority of people only knew the Zhengzhou Xinzheng International Airport, or the Xinzheng International Airport. Nowadays, the rapid development road of "opening up by aviation" is blazed out. People in the zone can easily go anywhere by airplane, high-speed train, subway and expressway. Not only people, but the goods can move freely. The prosperity and convenience there make people feel like they are in a port city.

I. The Central Plains Opening-up via Aviation

When night falls, the 3600-meter runway of the Xinzheng International Airport is spotted with the navigation lights like stars, where roaring planes are taxiing and taking off constantly, stimulating the heartbeat. The airport has already become a sleepless city.

Airport, as a gateway, represents the development level of a city and even the whole region to a certain extent. More than 20 years ago, the brand-new Xinzheng International Airport was completed and opened to navigation. The Central Plains, although in the inland, have got wings to fly since then. For more than 20 years, the airport runway has been narrowing the distance between Zhengzhou and the world and has facilitated the travel of people there.

The CBD of Zhengdong New District, with many high-rise buildings and woven traffic, has become a window to showcase the urban construction of

新郑国际机场夜景
Nightscape of Xinzheng International Airport

1956年，波音727，世界上最受欢迎的民航客机之一，开启了方案论证，而远在大洋彼岸的燕庄机场也扩建完成开始营运，拥抱蓝天对河南人民而言不再只是梦。

这一年，燕庄机场开辟了郑州第一条地方航线——郑州至南阳航线，成为民航为郑州老百姓服务的开端。由于工作需要常驻广州的缘故，身为一个郑州人，广州成为张为民的第二个家。"当时从郑州飞广州的机票要一两百元，而我一个月工资才30元。"回想起刚步入工作岗位时的情况，已经退休在家的老张不禁感叹道："在我们那个年代，坐一次飞机是不少河南人民的奢望。"运营当年，燕庄机场的旅客量仅12人次，货邮发送量仅793千克。随着改革开放的不断深入，民航业务的发展步伐逐步加快，航线增多，业务愈发繁忙，已运营30余年的燕庄机场越来越满足不了城市蓬勃发展的需要，成为郑州乃至河南对外交往和经济发展的一大制约，谋划建设新的机场迫在眉睫。

Zhengzhou and Henan. However, in the 1950s, this area was still a rolling sand dune where Zhengzhou Yanzhuang Airport, or Yanzhuang Airport, the earliest airport in Zhengzhou, was built here.

In 1956, Boeing 727, one of the most popular civil airliners in the world, started the deliberation for approval, while Yanzhuang Airport was expanded and started to operate, achieving the dream of embracing the blue sky for Henan people.

This year, Yanzhuang Airport opened Zhengzhou's first local route from Zhengzhou to Nanyang, making it a start for civil aviation to serve Zhengzhou people. Due to staying in Guangzhou for work, Zhang Weimin, a Zhengzhou native, takes Guangzhou as his second home. "At that time, the air ticket from Zhengzhou to Guangzhou cost one or two hundred *yuan*, and my monthly salary was only 30 *yuan*." Recalling the days when he took his first job, Mr. Zhang, now a retiree at home, cannot help sighing: "In our days, it is the luxury of many Henan people to take a plane." In the operation year, Yanzhuang Airport had only 12 passengers and only 793 kilograms of cargo and mail. With the continuous deepening of reform and opening up, the pace of civil aviation business development has gradually accelerated, routes have increased, and business has become busier and busier. Yanzhuang Airport, which has been in operation for more than 30 years, has become increasingly unable to meet the needs of the city's vigorous development and has become a significant constraint on Zhengzhou and even Henan's economic development, and foreign exchanges. Planning to build a new airport is imminent.

"The construction of the new international airport was listed as the 'No.1 Project' of the year, and the people of Henan must tighten their belts to build an international airport." From the very beginning of the site selection, the construction did not go smooth. All were needed to take into consideration, including the influence of wind direction on the runway, noise on the city, and how the new airport supported the development on the city. Cui Wei, the executive deputy commander of Xinzheng International Airport Construction Headquarters, fell into deep thoughts while mentioning the difficulties. After countless discussions and examinations with experts, the most comprehensive consideration was about to come. Finally, Xuedian Town, Xinzheng, the new site

"建设新机场当年被列为'1号工程',河南人民扎紧裤腰带也要建一个国际机场。"从选址伊始,新机场的建设就颇费周折:建设跑道要考虑风向、噪音对城市的影响,新机场如何协同配合城市发展……经历的困难,曾任新郑国际机场建设指挥部常务副指挥长的崔巍深有感触。会同多方专家,一次次讨论,一遍遍论证,只为最周全的考虑。200多个方案,最终位于郑州市东南方向的新郑薛店镇成功赢得新机场选址落地。

二十多年的发展更是见证了这一决策的前瞻性,郑州市区不断发展扩容,机场在这里有足够的空间大显身手。

1994年,投资十多亿元的新郑国际机场动工兴建,于1997年8月28日建成通航,机场搬了"新家",燕庄机场也逐渐退出舞台,成为郑州民航业发展历史中的一抹亮彩。

根据设计规划,新郑国际机场年旅客吞吐量可达380万人次,是燕庄机场最大吞吐负荷的3倍;每周可安排800余个航班,是燕庄机场最大安排量的4倍,具备接纳波音747等大型客机的能力。

曾有人形容,修机场就像给孩子做衣服,"甚至没怎么穿就小了"。随着河南发展的脚步大幅迈进,通航短短几年的新郑国际机场就成为"一件穿小的衣服"——2006年,机场吞吐量提前达到设计能力的"极限"。2007年12月29日,新郑国际机场改扩建工程竣工。旧貌换新颜,郑州民航发展再次跨入新的历史起点。

扩建工程投入使用后,机场航站楼面积由从前的45900平方米增加到128899平方米,可满足年旅客吞吐量1150万人次、货邮吞吐量35万吨。2008年,新郑国际机场被国家民航局确定为中国八大区域性枢纽机场之一。

从2010年起,新郑国际机场客货运量飞速增长。截至2013年年底,机场旅客吞吐量完成1206万人次,货邮吞吐量完成21.4万吨,增幅排名全国第一。迅猛的发展速度又使得刚扩建完成的新郑国际机场达到饱

located in the southeast of Zhengzhou, beat other more than 200 plans.

The development of more than 20 years has witnessed the forward-looking nature of this decision. As Zhengzhou has been expanding, the airport has enough space to show its talents here.

In 1994, Xinzheng International Airport, with an investment of more than one billion *yuan*, started the construction and was opened to traffic on August 28, 1997. The airport moved to a "new home", which was a bright chapter in Zhengzhou's civil aviation history, and then Yanzhuang Airport gradually withdrew from the stage.

According to the design plan, the annual passenger throughput of the new airport could reach 3.8 million, which is three times the maximum throughput of Yanzhuang Airport; More than 800 flights could be arranged every week, which is four times that of Yanzhuang Airport. The airport also could accept Boeing 747 and other large passenger aircraft.

It was said that repairing an airport was like making clothes for a child, as it was quickly to be small before wearing for a long while. Due to the rapid development of Henan, Xinzheng International Airport became "a piece of small clothes" after only a few years, as the airport throughput reached the maximum designed capacity ahead of schedule in 2006.On December 29, 2007, its expansion was completed. Zhengzhou's civil aviation entered a new starting point again.

After the expansion project is put into use, the area of the airport terminal has increased from 45,900 square meters to 128,899 square meters, with annual passenger throughput reaching 11.5 million passengers and cargo and mail throughput, 350,000 tons. In 2008, the Airport was identified by the Civil Aviation Administration of China as one of China's eight major regional hub airports.

Since 2010, the passenger and freight volume of Xinzheng International Airport have increased rapidly. By the end of 2013, the airport had handled 12.06 million passengers and 214,000 tons of cargo and mail, ranking first in China. The rapid development speed made the newly expanded Xinzheng International Airport seem small again. In 2013, the Zhengzhou Airport Economy Zone was approved by the State Council. The airport, located at the core of the zone, embarked on a new course of rapid development by virtue of opportunities of the

新郑国际机场候机大厅
The Departure Lounge of Xinzheng International Airport

和。2013年，航空港实验区获国务院批准设立。位于航空港实验区核心位置的新郑国际机场，乘着国家战略的东风，开启了迅猛发展的新历程。2015年新郑国际机场T2航站楼启用，机场正式进入双跑道、双航站楼时代。航空港实验区发展也再添新动力。

自1997年8月通航以来，新郑国际机场年旅客吞吐量由通航之初的100多万人次提升至2020年的2140.67万人次。现如今，新郑国际机场3周的客运量就相当于20年前全年的客运量；与此同时，新郑国际机场2020年货邮吞吐量达到63.94万吨，保持中部"双第一"。

national strategy. In 2015, its Terminal 2 opened, marking the airport officially entered the era of double runways and double terminals. The zone was injected with new impetus.

Since it opened in August 1997, the airport has increased the annual passenger throughput from more than 1 million passengers at the beginning to 21.4067 million in 2020. Nowadays, the passenger traffic in three weeks is equivalent to that of the whole year 20 years ago. At the same time, the cargo and mail throughput reached 639,400 tons in 2020. Both indicators have seen the airport at the top place.

新郑国际机场一派繁忙
The Busy Xinzheng International Airport

On November 18, 2020, Civil Aviation Trends Conference 2020 was held in Zhengzhou where a set of airport data was quite eye-catching. There were 31 cargo airlines (24 in international regions), 51 cargo routes (41 in international regions) and 63 navigable cities (46 in international regions), reaching 11 countries along the Belt and Road Initiative and 16 of the top 20 international aviation hubs; There were 54 passenger airlines (18 in international regions), 194 passenger routes (27 in international regions) and 130 navigable cities (24 in international regions). With planes coming and going and a denser and denser network of air routes, Xinzheng International Airport presents a magnificent picture of "carrying the world in by day and sending China out by night".

2020年11月18日,在郑州举行的2020民航趋势论坛上,新郑国际机场的一组数据颇为亮眼:运行的货运航空公司31家(国际地区24家),货运航线51条(国际地区41条),通航城市63个(国际地区46个),通达11个"一带一路"沿线国家,在全球前20位枢纽航点中已通达16个;客运航空公司54家(国际地区18家),客运航线194条(国际地区27条),通航城市130个(国际地区24个)。来来往往的飞机,越织越密的航线网络,新郑国际机场正上演着"白天把'世界'运进来,夜间把'中国'送出去"的壮美图景。

遥想当年,郑州航站作为中华人民共和国首个航站正式开通,那时的规划和建设者也许可以想到,半个多世纪后这座航站会变成一座国际机场,但他们恐怕想不到,从这座机场竟然"飞"出了一座国际航空新

空客A380降落新郑国际机场
Airbus A380 landed at Xinzheng International Airport.

Back then, Zhengzhou Terminal, the first officially opened terminal in China, could be expected to be international after more than half a century, but not to grow a new international aviation city. Who would have thought or dared to think about reaching the whole world?

On June 30, 2020, many aerial photography enthusiasts gathered at the Airport, looking forward to the arrival of a new guest. A white and blue figure slowly landing on the apron, was called Big Mac in the Air, also the hero of the day—Airbus A380. The guarantee of its successful arrival, the world's largest airliner, not only requires the close cooperation of airport staff, but also lays a solid foundation for improving hardware facilities of the airport.

"This is the first time that we have never dared to think of the possibility before." The moment the shutter was pressed, Wang Jianguo murmured. As a Zhengzhou native, Wang Jianguo has been paying close attention to the development of the Xinzheng International Airport. When he was talking about airplanes, his face was full of glow. When he was recalling the development in recent years, the Xinzheng International Airport Phase II Project was the most unforgettable for him. Surrounded by cheers from fellow photographers and breeze across his cheeks, Wang Jianguo was drowned into deep thoughts back to five years ago.

On December 22, 2015, Guo Gengmao, then secretary of Henan Provincial Party Committee, solemnly announced: "The Xinzheng International Airport Phase II Project was officially put into operation." This happy event that more than 100 million people in Henan have been looking forward to for a long time has finally arrived. It marks that Xinzheng International Airport has entered a new era of double runways and double terminals, which is of great significance for building a modern comprehensive transportation hub and an international logistic center. It is undoubtedly a milestone for the economic and the social development of Zhengzhou Airport Economy Zone and even Henan.

It took only ten months from the start of the second phase of the project to the beginning of construction; and only 24 months from the start of construction to the official commissioning. It was another well-known example of the Zhengzhou Airport Economy Zone speed and Zhengzhou speed."It was built so fast that it was different day by day." Mr. Zhang, whose home was near the

城。所谓"连天接地、通达全球",谁能想到,又有谁敢去想?

2020年6月30日,众多航空摄影爱好者齐聚新郑国际机场,翘首以盼一位新客人的到来。随着一个白蓝相间的身影缓缓降落在停机坪上,新郑国际机场终于迎来了今天的主人公——素有"空中巨无霸"之称的空客A380。成功保障全球最大客机空客A380,不仅需要机场工作人员的紧密配合,也为新郑国际机场完备硬件设施打下了坚实基础。

"这可是第一次啊,以前哪里敢想。"按下快门的那一刻,王建国喃喃道。身为一名老郑州,王建国一直都在关注着新郑国际机场的发展。谈起飞机,这位中原汉子脸上是抑制不住的光彩。回想起这几年的发展,新郑国际机场二期工程投运是最让他难忘的。身边是摄影同好们的欢呼,缕缕清风滑过脸颊,拉扯着王建国的思绪飘回到了五年前。

2015年12月22日,时任河南省委书记郭庚茂庄严宣布:"新郑国际机场二期工程正式投入运营。"这件河南省一亿多人民期盼已久的喜事终于到来,标志着新郑国际机场迈入了"双跑道、双航站楼"的新时代,这对打造现代综合交通枢纽和国际物流中心有着十分重要的意义,无疑是航空港实验区乃至河南省经济社会发展进程中的一座里程碑。

从二期工程启动到开工,仅仅用了10个月;从开工到正式投用,只用了24个月。为人称道的"港区速度""郑州速度"再次上演。"建得很快,简直就是一天一个样儿。"家就在机场附近的张大爷,和众多建设者一起,亲眼见证了新郑国际机场二期工程的华丽绽放。

急速之下,工程质量是否有保障?负责新郑国际机场二期工程监理的杨恒泰信心满满。工程质量,是监理单位不可推卸的责任。防止"豆腐渣"工程,保证工程质量,更是监理的职责所在。"李克强总理在考察新郑国际机场二期项目时,嘱托我们要确保工程质量,我们始终把质量二字铭记于心。"从工程伊始,杨恒泰就和所有监理人员立下了目标:获得素有"中国建筑界的奥斯卡"之称的鲁班奖。工期紧张,但也要高质量、高标准、高速度完成项目建设,是所有参建单位许下的誓言。"困

airport, has witnessed the gorgeous bloom of Phase II Project together with many builders.

Was the quality of the project guaranteed at such speed? Yang Hengtai, who was in charge of the supervision of Phase II Project, was full of confidence. Engineering quality was the unshakable responsibility of supervision units. It was the responsibility of the supervisor to ensure the project quality and prevent the tofu project. "When Premier Li Keqiang inspected the Phase II Project, he asked us to ensure the quality that we always kept in mind." From the beginning, Yang Hengtai and all supervisors set the goal: To win the Luban Award, known as the "Oscar of Chinese Architecture". The construction period was tight, but it was the oath made by all participating units to complete the project construction with high quality, high standard and high speed. "In front of me, there is no difficulty in the way!" The slogan was full of enthusiasm and beans to win the lofty ambition!

Against the darkness lighted shortly by the fireworks, the laughter of the whole family sitting together seemed to be heard nearby. It was a day for a family reunion, but all the builders of the second phase of Xinzheng International Airport were busy mixing sand, pouring cement, and tying steel bars. There were no holidays, regardless of the cold weather. During the Spring Festival, an average of 2,344 people stuck to the construction every day. The busy figures with no regrets became the brightest scenery of the airport. Finally, when the last node of schedule was completed, they all smiled like children.

On November 6, 2017, Xinzheng International Airport Phase II Expansion Project, including Terminal 2, Comprehensive Transportation Transfer Center and Tower Community, won Luban Award. Seeing the good news in the newspaper, all the builders were excited. Their goal has been achieved, which was the highest praise for all efforts.

In the Phase II Project, Terminal 2 was the core, whose height was 107 meters, three times larger than Terminal 1. After completion, parking spaces have increased from 47 to 78, the passenger throughput to 29 million passengers, and the cargo and mail throughput to 500,000 tons. With the newly built 4F-class runway with the length of 3600 meters and the width of 60 meters, Xinzheng International Airport has gained a brand-new growth space.

In front of Terminal 2, the GTC Airport Comprehensive Transportation

难面前有我在，我的面前无困难！"口号声中，是满腔热血，是全力以赴，是必胜的壮志与豪情！

阵阵绚丽的烟花在远处一闪而过，只留下天地之间一瞬的明亮，耳畔似乎能听见全家围坐一起的欢笑。本是阖家团圆的日子，新郑国际机场二期的所有建设者们却忙着搅拌沙子、浇筑水泥、绑扎钢筋。没有节假日，不顾天寒，春节期间平均每天2344人坚守一线施工。忙碌的身影成为机场最亮眼的风景线，无怨无悔。终于，最后一个节点完工，他们像孩子那样，满脸笑颜。

2017年11月6日，"新郑国际机场二期扩建工程(T2航站楼、综合交通换乘中心及塔台小区)荣获鲁班奖"。看着报纸上的喜讯，所有建设者倍感振奋。他们的目标实现了，这是对所有付出的最高褒奖。

在二期工程中，T2航站楼是核心，107米的设计高度足足比T1航站楼大了三倍。建成后，停机位将由现有的47个增加至78个，客运吞吐量提高到2900万人次，货邮吞吐量提升到50万吨，伴随着新修的一条3600米×60米4F级跑道，新郑国际机场获得了全新的成长空间。

在T2航站楼前方，地下4层、地上2层的"GTC机场综合交通换乘中心"是此次新郑国际机场二期工程的另一重点，也是继上海虹桥机场后，全国第二个将多种交通方式有效衔接的综合换乘中心。充分利用更多竖向垂直换乘方式，垂直布局，引入高速铁路、城际铁路、城市轨道交通、高速公路等多种交通运输方式，新郑国际机场将成为具备空陆联运条件，实现客运"零距离换乘"和货运"无缝衔接"的现代综合交通枢纽。

从地上到地下，这项浩大的工程，仿若庄子笔下的鲲鹏，蓄势待发，"怒而飞，其翼若垂天之云"，稳稳地落在这片昔日的原野上。

若说T2航站楼和GTC机场综合交通换乘中心，撑起了新郑国际机场二期工程"巨无霸"的称号，那么被河南人民称为"笛塔"的空中塔台，使这个"巨无霸"多了些柔情的意味。

Transfer Center with 4 floors underground and 2 floors on the ground, was another focus of Phase II Project, which was the second comprehensive transfer center that effectively connects many ways of transportation in China after Shanghai Hongqiao Airport. The center makes full use of more vertical transfer modes like introducing high-speed railway, inter-city railway, urban rail transit and expressway. Thus, the airport, as an air-land transportation hub, realizes zero-distance transfer for passengers and seamless connection for cargo.

From the ground to underground, this huge project, like Kunpeng described by Zhuangzi that a miles-large bird can rocket to the sky, stands firmly in the farmland.

新郑国际机场全景
Panorama of Xinzheng International Airport

曾有人言说,建筑是文化的容器,承载着文化传承和推广的使命。新郑国际机场空管塔台便是如此。作为飞机起降指令的传递者,93米多高,造型别致、独具韵味的空管塔台,于繁华之中独添一丝缥缈。

1987年,在河南省舞阳县一处石器时代遗址——贾湖村遗址,出土了两件通体土黄、晶莹剔透的文物,这就是令世人瞩目的贾湖骨笛。悠悠岁月,8000多年的时光沉淀,贾湖骨笛比古埃及出现的笛子早2000年,为世界笛子的鼻祖。结合中原文化传承和中原人外柔内刚的性格秉性,修长优美、造型流畅的贾湖骨笛,化身成为新郑国际机场的空管塔台,带着中原大地腾飞的梦想,与往来起降的飞机,一起奏响新时代郑州航空港澎湃发展的魅力乐章。

飞抵新郑国际机场的卢货航飞机正在卸货
Luxembourg Cargo Airplanes are unloading cargo at Xinzheng International Airport.

"卢森堡航空730,郑州塔台……可以落地。"伴着初升的朝阳,一条条空管指令,又打开了全新的一天,而属于郑州的航空故事,还在继续上演。

2011年客运量破千万,2016年客运量破两千万……一组组数字,

If Terminal 2 and GTC Airport Comprehensive Transportation Transfer Center win the title of "Big Mac" for Phase II Project, the air tower called "Flute Tower" by Henan people brings warmth to the title.

It has been said that architecture, a container of culture, bears the mission of cultural inheritance and promotion. So is the air traffic control tower. For sending the instructions of taking off and landing for airplanes, the tower, more than 93 meters high, has a unique shape and charm, adding some mystery to the prosperity of a city.

In 1987, two pieces of yellow and crystal clear cultural relics were unearthed at Jiahu Village Site, a Stone Age site in Wuyang County, Henan. These are the Jiahu bone flute that attracted worldwide attention. They are over 8,000 years old, 2000 years more than similar ones in Egypt, now the originator of flute in the world. Combining culture and personality of local people in the Central Plains, the tower takes the same slender and graceful shape as Jiahu bone flute blowing the dream of surging development of Zhengzhou Airport in the new era together with the planes taking off and landing.

"CLX 730 Zhengzhou Tower, cleared to land." With the rising sun, the day

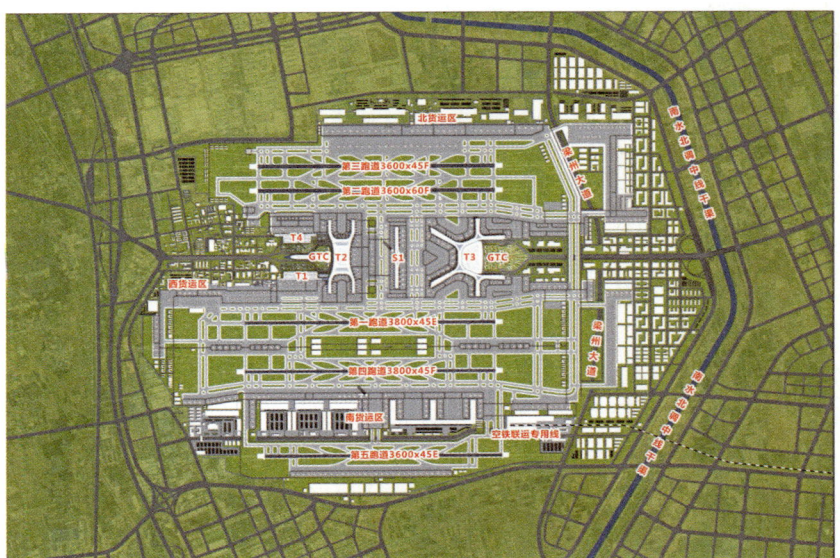

新郑国际机场总体规划图
Overall Planning Map of Xinzheng International Airport

是新郑国际机场蓬勃发展的有力见证，更是其与航空港实验区如火如荼建设同频共振的鲜活证明。不断刷新、逆势飘红的数据，也让新郑国际机场三期工程开始提上日程。

2020年4月16日，航空港实验区又迎喜讯。新郑国际机场北货运区工程、中国邮政郑州航空邮件处理中心项目开工仪式举行，标志着新郑国际机场三期工程建设正式启动。这一刻，新郑国际机场迈开新步伐，欲扶摇直上，振翅翱翔。

从富士康落地、郑州新郑综合保税区运行，到航空港实验区获国务院批准设立，每一个重要节点，新郑国际机场始终处于核心位置。2020年，新郑国际机场完成货邮吞吐量63.94万吨，成功跨越60万吨大关；完成旅客吞吐量2140.67万人次。在新冠疫情影响下，2020年新郑国际机场客、货运量分别超越南京禄口国际机场和成都双流国际机场，晋升至国内第11位和第6位，连续4年保持中部机场"双第一"……

不靠海、不沿边，展开双翼向蓝天，古老的中原大地触摸着五彩斑斓的外部世界，中原人的"飞天梦"也正在一步步变为现实。

begins with one instruction after another, telling the stories of Zhengzhou aviation.

Passenger capacity exceeded 10 million passengers in 2011 and 20 million in 2016. These figures were strong supports to the vigorous development of the airport and to its joint construction of the Zhengzhou Airport Economy Zone. The upward figures reminded of starting Phase III Project.

On April 16, 2020, out came another piece of good news about the Zhengzhou Airport Economy Zone. The commencement ceremony of Xinzheng International Airport North Cargo Area Project and China Post Zhengzhou Air Mail Processing Center Project was held, marking that Xinzheng International Airport Phase III Project kicked off. Since then, Xinzheng International Airport has taken a new stride onward.

From the landing of Foxconn, to operation of Zhengzhou Xinzheng Comprehensive Bonded Zone, and the approval of the Zhengzhou Airport Economy Zone by the State Council, the airport has always been determined as the core of each event. In 2020, the airport's cargo and mail throughput reached 639,400 tons, crossing the 600,000-ton mark. The passenger throughput was 21.4067 million passengers. Despite the shock of COVID-19 pandemic, in 2020, the airport surpassed Nanjing Lukou International Airport and Chengdu Shuangliu International Airport and ranked the 11th and 6th places in China in terms of the passenger and freight volume respectively, maintaining the double first among the airports in Central China for four consecutive years.

Not alongside the sea or the border, the Central Plains connect with the wonderful outside world by air, together with achieving its aviation dream step by step.

二、"贴地飞行"通八方

2020年元旦,新年的第一缕阳光照亮了航空港实验区,在紧锣密鼓施工的铁路郑州南站项目现场,一列由中国自主研发制造、完全拥有自主知识产权的"复兴号"高速动车组列车从站内呼啸而过,它的目的地是距离郑州东站九百多千米外的上海虹桥站。从郑州乘坐这趟"贴地飞行"的列车,经由郑阜高铁到上海虹桥仅需5小时17分,比既有线运行时间最短的"传统"火车还要快三个半小时以上。

"复兴号"列车驶过建设中的郑州南站
A Rejuvenation train is passing by unfinished Zhengzhou South Railway Station.

2020年12月12日,汉字"米"字形的郑州高铁枢纽建设再传喜讯:郑州至太原高速铁路,新郑国际机场至郑州南站城际铁路正式开通。在此之前,从航空港实验区去往西北方向的太原,首先要到郑州乘车,接着在郑州换乘到太原的"传统"火车需要在此基础上再运行12个多小时;高铁由于需绕行石家庄,则要再运行4个多小时。郑太高铁开通后,航

II. Flying High-speed Trains to All Directions

The first day of 2020 saw the first ray of sunshine illuminate the Zhengzhou Airport Economy Zone where the Zhengzhou South Railway Station construction site was passed by Rejuvenation high-speed train independently developed and manufactured by China, whose destination was Shanghai Hongqiao Railway Station, more than 900 kilometers away from Zhengzhou East Railway Station. The Zhengzhou-Fuyang high-speed train took only 5 hours and 17 minutes from Zhengzhou to Shanghai Hongqiao, three and a half hours less than the fastest traditional train.

On December 12, 2020, out came the good news about constructing the star-shaped high-speed train network with Zhengzhou as the hub: Zhengzhou-Taiyuan High-speed Railway and Intercity Railway from Xinzheng International Airport to Zhengzhou South Railway Station were officially opened. For heading from the Zhengzhou Airport Economy Zone to Taiyuan in the northwest, one needed to arrive first from Zhengzhou in the traditional train to Taiyuan for another over 12 hours. Also, the high-speed train took another over 4 hours because it needed to bypass Shijiazhuang first before arriving in Taiyuan. The opening of Zhengzhou-Taiyuan high-speed train reduced the time needed where one took the bullet train in the airport and seamlessly transferred to the high-speed train heading to Taiyuan. The whole journey took only over 3 hours at the soonest, which made it convenient for Henan people and Shanxi people to travel and exchange.

The opening of the intercity railway from the underground of Terminal 2 of the airport to Zhengzhou South Railway Station is also of great significance. This section of the railway has a length of 10.9 kilometers, connecting three high-speed railways including Zhengzhou-Taiyuan, Zhengzhou-Chongqing and Zhengzhou-Fuyang routes. It also links Zhengzhou Railway Station, Xinzheng International Airport Station and Zhengzhou South Railway Station, meeting the travel demand of passengers from the three routes to the airport by zero transfer between airplane and bullet train. It strengthens the connection between the airport and Zhengzhou high-speed rail hub, consolidating the advantages of

空港实验区去往太原的运行时间有了明显缩短,从铁路新郑国际机场站乘坐动车组,到达郑州站不出站即可换乘开往太原方向的高铁,全程最快仅需 3 个多小时,豫晋两地群众的出行和交流更加高效便捷。

郑州南站效果图
Effect Drawing of Zhengzhou South Railway Station

新郑国际机场至郑州南站城际铁路的开通也意义非凡,这段由新郑国际机场 T2 航站楼地下向郑州南站引出的铁路全长 10.9 千米,连通了郑太、郑渝、郑阜三条高铁,实现了郑州站与新郑国际机场站、郑州南站之间的无缝衔接,满足了上述三条高铁沿途旅客到新郑国际机场"空铁零换乘"的出行需求,强化了新郑国际机场与郑州高铁枢纽的联络,航空港实验区的综合交通枢纽优势进一步显现,城市的高质量发展得到

the Zhengzhou Airport Economy Zone as a comprehensive transportation hub and sound development of Zhengzhou.

城际铁路列车在航空港实验区穿城而过
A intercity railway train passed through the Zhengzhou Airport Economy Zone.

Looking back, in the early 20th century, the Lugouqiao-Hankou Railway (now the Beijing-Guangzhou Railway) and Lanzhou-Lianyungang Railway met in Zhengzhou, boosting the rise of Zhengzhou and blazing the trail of being prosperous, superior and strong by transportation advantage. After entering the 21st century, Beijing-Guangzhou High-speed Railway and Xuzhou-Lanzhou High-speed Railway, which run almost parallel to the two Railways mentioned above, also met in Zhengzhou. The newly-built Zhengzhou East Railway Station has become one of the new focuses to promote the development of Zhengzhou's main urban area, especially the eastern region. These not only improved Zhengzhou transportation, but also accelerated the formation of a new economic circle and daily life circle, which expanded the urban framework of Zhengzhou, its radius of urban economic radiation, the comprehensive strength and influence.

Today, with the basic completion of star-shaped high-speed rail network, the Zhengzhou Airport Economy Zone located at the crux takes off by high-speed train and airplane. Also, Zhengzhou South Railway Station, the second

了强力推动。

　　回望过去，20世纪初，卢汉铁路（现京广铁路既有线）、陇海铁路在郑州交会，让郑州这座"火车拉来的城市"快速兴起，开辟了一条"因交通而兴、因交通而优、因交通而强"的发展道路。进入21世纪，分别与京广铁路、陇海铁路近乎平行走向的京广高铁、徐兰高铁在郑州交会，新建的郑州东站成为拉动郑州主城区尤其是东部区域发展的新着力点之一。两座铁路特等客运站带给郑州的不仅是交通条件的改善，也包括了城市新经济圈、生活圈的形成，在拉大郑州城市框架的同时，扩大了城市经济辐射半径，提升了城市的综合实力和影响力。

　　今天，随着郑州"米"字形高铁网络基本建成，处在"米"字路口关键位置的航空港实验区也借助"高铁+航空"，插上了新时代"腾飞"的翅膀，迎来了郑州南站这一中国国内站场规模第二大的铁路客运站项目，迎来了综合交通枢纽建设的新机遇。郑州南站，这座集高铁客运中心、高铁物流中心、"空铁"换乘中心、长途客运中心和旅游集散中心于一体的车站，建成后将与新郑国际机场联袂构成"空铁"双核驱动发展的优越格局，进一步强化航空港实验区乃至河南省在全国综合交通枢纽的中心地位，扩充航空港实验区腹地范围和口岸通关能力，更好地服务于中国（河南）自由贸易试验区建设，成为推动河南经济发展，让中原更加出彩的新引擎。

　　来到航空港实验区，从新郑国际机场向东南7千米左右，就是正在建设的郑州南站项目现场。郑州南站是郑州市第三座大型综合铁路客运枢纽站，未来将与郑州站、郑州东站形成"金三角"的格局，在串起"米"字形高速铁路网和中原城市群城际铁路网的同时，也将新郑国际机场与郑州铁路枢纽更加紧密地联系在一起。郑州南站是"米"字"撇"和"捺"即郑渝高铁的中间站、郑阜高铁的起始站，也是中原城市群城际铁路的中心站、换乘站。通过郑阜高铁，可以直接通达中国东部的杭州，通过郑渝高铁则直接深入中国西南的重庆。同时，由郑州南站向北还可连通

largest railway passenger station project in China, brings new opportunities for the construction of a comprehensive transportation hub. Zhengzhou South Railway Station, which plays the role as the passenger transport center, rail logistics center of high-speed train, air-rail transfer center, long-distance passenger transport center and tourist distribution center, will combine with the airport to form a superior development pattern supported by aviation and rail after its accomplishment, so as to further strengthen the central position of the Zhengzhou Airport Economy Zone and Henan in the national comprehensive transportation hub, and to expand the hinterland scope and clearance capacity of the zone. It will better serve the construction of China (Henan) Pilot Free Trade Zone as well as Henan's economic development as a new engine.

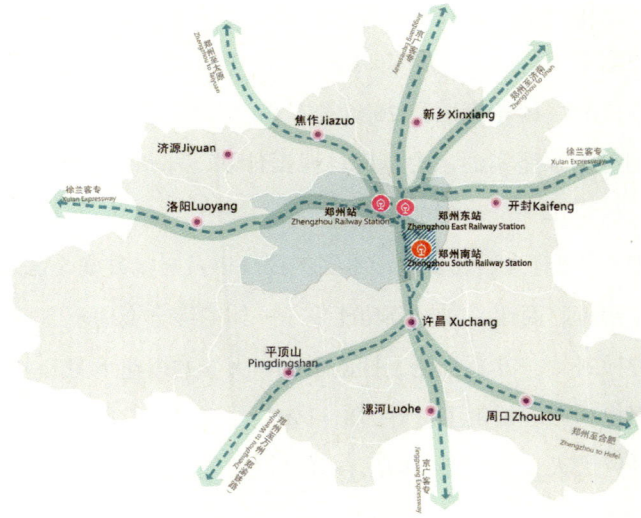

通达八个方向的"米"字形高铁网络示意图
Diagram of Star-shaped High-speed Rail Network in Eight Directions

At the zone, about 7 kilometers southeast from Xinzheng International Airport, is the Zhengzhou South Railway Station under construction. Zhengzhou South Railway Station is the third large-scale comprehensive railway passenger transport hub station in Zhengzhou. In the future, it will form a "Golden Triangle" pattern with Zhengzhou Station and Zhengzhou East Railway Station. The pattern also links the radial high-speed railway network and the intercity railway

"米"字"横""竖"以及其余两个"点",即郑西高铁、京广高铁、郑太高铁和正在建设的郑济高铁。"贴地飞行,通达八方",航空港实验区这个综合交通枢纽就是这么豪横。

作为中国站场规模第二大的火车站,郑州南站的主要工程包括建筑面积48.3万平方米的站房工程,总规模为16座站台32条到发线的站场工程,郑州南动车所工程以及与郑州南站配套的地铁土建工程、市政配套应急工程、机登洛城际应急工程等。

2020年11月5日10时18分,随着重达3200吨、面积31800平方米的钢结构屋盖第三区域钢桁架精准落位,郑州南站主站房顺利封顶。目前,这座郑州最大的"毛坯房"开始逐步转入"装修"阶段。同步建设的郑州南动车所已于2021年1月10日开门"营业",新建的6线检修库、临修库、镟轮库以及26线存车场全部投用,这也为日后郑州南站的投用打下了坚实的运力基础。根据计划,郑州南站将于2022年建成并投入运营。

现如今,随着人们物质生活水平的提高以及对精神文化需求的增加,将换乘、物流、商业、文娱等功能集于一体的综合交通枢纽模式备受青睐。这种模式,一方面有利于打造现代、大气的枢纽形象和城市形象,另一方面也为旅客提供了良好的出行体验。面对今后航空港实验区发展所带来的巨大人流量,郑州南站在设计之初就充分考虑到了旅客高效换乘的实际需求。例如,在旅客进出站通道的设计上,郑州南站采取了"下进下出、上进下出、腰部多口进站"的多维立体进站模式,保障旅客能在更近的距离以更短的时间从容进站乘车。

根据设计,郑州南站地面层的出站厅以及快速进站厅,均预留了与地铁的直通条件。未来,这里将具备地铁和高铁安检互认的条件,旅客无须出站也无须多次安检即可实现换乘,大大节约了宝贵时间。整合了高铁、城铁、地铁、公交、出租、长途巴士等各类交通要素,来到航空港实验区,在郑州南站,你所能想到的、用到的出行方式都能"零换乘"。

network of the Central Plains urban agglomeration. Thus, the airport links more closely with Zhengzhou railway hub. Zhengzhou South Railway Station is the intermediate station of Zhengzhou-Chongqing High-speed Railway, the starting station of Zhengzhou-Fuyang High-speed Railway, and the central station and transfer station of inter-city railway of the Central Plains urban agglomeration. Through the Zhengzhou-Fuyang High-speed Railway, you can directly reach Hangzhou in the eastern China, and Chongqing in southwest China through the Zhengzhou-Chongqing High-speed Railway. At the same time, it also meets Zhengzhou-Xi'an High-speed Railway, Beijing-Guangzhou High-speed Railway, Zhengzhou-Taiyuan High-speed Railway and Zhengzhou-Jinan High-speed Railway under construction. Flying high-speed trains is accessible in all directions,

郑州南站空铁换乘中心效果图
Effect Drawing of Air-rail Transfer Center of Zhengzhou South Railway Station

郑州南站长途客运中心效果图

Effect Drawing of Long-distance Bus Station of Zhengzhou South Railway Station

来到一座城市，其火车站的现代化程度通常也折射出这座城市的整体发展水平。现在，自动闸机、自助售票机、饮水机、无障碍电梯以及智能化洗手间等一系列人性化服务设施正陆续成为各地火车站房内的标配。作为航空港实验区城市发展的一大新亮点，新建的郑州南站在拥有这些的同时，还智慧地将站房地暖与中央空调系统相结合，根据温度和湿度自动调节空调系统的水温、风量。值得一提的是，郑州南站的地暖系统不但能在冬天发挥"暖"的作用，在炎夏，地暖系统的管道里会注入20℃左右的水，促进站房内部的温度调节，增加旅客候车时的体感舒适度，带给旅客家一般的感觉。

and the comprehensive transportation hub of the Zhengzhou Airport Economy Zone is so exquisite.

As the second largest railway station in China, the main projects of Zhengzhou South Railway Station include the station building project with a construction area of 483,000 square meters, the station project with a total scale of 16 platforms and 32 arrival and departure lines, the Zhengzhou South EMU project, the subway civil engineering supporting Zhengzhou South Railway Station, the municipal supporting emergency project, the Zhengzhou Airport-Dengfeng-Luoyang inter-city emergency project and others.

At 10∶18 on November 5, 2020, with the precise placement of the steel truss in the third area of the steel roof weighing 3,200 tons and covering an area of 31,800 square meters, the main station building of Zhengzhou South Railway Station was successfully capped. At present, the largest non-decorated building in Zhengzhou has been gradually decorated. Zhengzhou South High-speed Railway Station, which was built simultaneously, opened to the public on January 10, 2021. All the newly-built 6-line maintenance depots, temporary repair depots and wheel depots, as well as 26-line depots were put into use, which also laid a solid capacity foundation for the operation of Zhengzhou South Railway Station in the future. According to the plan, Zhengzhou South Railway Station will be completed and put into operation in 2022.

Nowadays, with the improvement of people's material living standards and the increase of spiritual and cultural needs, the comprehensive transportation hub mode is favored, integrating transfer, logistics, commerce, entertainment and other functions into one. This mode, on the one hand, is conducive to creating a modern and magnificent image of hub and city; on the other hand, it also provides passengers with good travel experience. Facing the huge flow of people brought about by the development of the Zhengzhou Airport Economy Zone in the future, Zhengzhou South Railway Station fully considered the actual demand of efficient passenger transfer at the beginning of its design. For example, in the design of passengers' entrance and exit passages, Zhengzhou South Railway Station would adopt a multi-dimensional entrance mode of entering from Floor 1 and Floor 3 to Floor 2, and exiting to Floor 1, so as to ensure that passengers can get in easily at a closer distance and in a shorter time.

第一章 交通大枢纽

建设中的郑州南站
Zhengzhou South Railway Station is under construction.

自航空港实验区获批成立以来，现代物流业的发展一直被摆在十分重要的位置。近年来，基于高铁网络的持续加密，依托高铁的快速物流系统正在推进实用化，郑州南站显然顺应了这一发展趋势，配套了高铁物流中心。在细节上，为了更好地捋顺物流的"最后一千米"，郑州南站为每一座站台都预设了车辆通道，这在国内以往的火车站是少有的设计，极大地方便了各类车辆的进出。加之车站与新郑国际机场相距仅7千米左右，通过多种交通方式实现航空运输与铁路运输的良好衔接和优势互补，无疑将促进航空港实验区形成"1+1＞2"的产业联通效应。

According to the design, its exit hall and the fast entrance hall on the ground floor have reserved direct access to the subway. In the future, there will be mutual recognition of security checks between subway and high-speed train without need to leave the station and to have multiple checks for transfer, greatly saving precious time. It integrates all means of transportation that you can think and use, such as high-speed train, inter-city rail, subway, public transportation, taxi, long-distance bus, to achieve zero transfer to arrive in the Zhengzhou Airport Economy Zone.

When you come to a city, the modernity of its railway station usually reflects the overall development of the city. At present, a series of humanized service facilities, such as automatic gates, self-service ticket vending machines, drinking fountains, barrier-free elevators and intelligent toilets, are becoming standard facilities in railway stations across China. As a new highlight in the urban development of the zone, the newly-built Zhengzhou South Railway Station will also be equipped with the floor heating and central air conditioning system, intelligently and automatically adjusting the water temperature and air volume of the system according to the temperature and humidity. It is worth mentioning that the floor heating system can not only warm people in winter, but also adjust temperature by injecting about 20℃ water into the pipes of the system in summer, for increasing the comfort of passengers when they are waiting for the train, and making passengers feel at home.

Since the establishment of the Zhengzhou Airport Economy Zone, the development of modern logistics industry has been placed in a critical position. In recent years, the rapid logistics system relying on the denser high-speed train network is to be more practical. Zhengzhou South Railway Station obviously follows this trend to build the high-speed rail logistics center. In detail, in order to better connect the last mile of logistics, the station has preset vehicle passages for each platform, which is rare to be seen in China before and greatly facilitates the entry and exit of all kinds of vehicles. In addition, the station is only about 7 kilometers away from Xinzheng International Airport. Connecting and supporting each other by various other means of transportation, Zhengzhou South Railway Station will undoubtedly promote the industrial connectivity effect of "1 +1 > 2" in the Zhengzhou Airport Economy Zone.

三、连天接地"零距离"

在一片"空白"处创造新的天地,白纸绘新图的梦想离不开交通运输线的"勾勒"。自航空港实验区获批成立以来,这里的交通一直在争分夺秒地持续建设发展。航空港实验区要实现人畅其行,物畅其流,必然要发挥新郑国际机场综合交通换乘中心功能,实现机场与高速铁路、高速公路等的无缝衔接。大枢纽体系下,高速铁路、高速公路主要服务国内旅客、货物运输;枢纽机场的空运则侧重国际运输、国内长途运输。这种连天接地、无缝衔接的优势,将有力拓展航空港实验区交通枢纽的辐射范围,提高运输效能。

"复兴号"列车驶过航空港实验区
A Rejuvenation train is passing by the Zhengzhou Airport Economy Zone.

相对航空和铁路,公路在打通"最后一千米"方面有着其天然的优势。航空港实验区境内有着密集的市政路网,高速公路也可谓四通八

III. Zero Distance Transfer Between Air and Rail Transportation

To create a new world from scratch is a dream that cannot be achieved without the support of transportation. Since the establishment of the Zhengzhou Airport Economy Zone was approved, the traffic there has been racing against time to develop. To realize the smooth movement of passengers and goods in the zone, it is necessary to give full play to the function of Xinzheng International Airport's comprehensive transportation transfer center for seamless connection among the airport, high-speed railways and expressways. Under the large hub system, high-speed railways and expressways mainly serve domestic passenger and cargo transportation. Air transportation at hub airport focuses on international business and domestic long-haul transportation. This advantage of seamless connection between air and rail transportation will effectively expand the radiation range of the hub in the zone and improve the transportation efficiency.

Compared with aviation and railways, highways have their natural advantages in connecting the last mile. There is a dense municipal road network and expressways in the zone towards all directions. Beijing-Hong Kong-Macao Expressway, Shangqiu-Dengfeng Expressway, Anyang-Luoshan Expressway and other expressways, as well as G107 and G310, all meet there, seamlessly connecting with the Xinzheng International Airport and Zhengzhou South Railway Station. At present, the 1,000-kilometer truck routes basically cover the two world-class urban agglomerations, namely the Beijing-Tianjin-Hebei and Yangtze River Delta, and Guanzhong Urban Agglomeration and Bohai Rim Economic Circle.

For supporting the layout of expressway network, in recent years, the expressway entrances and exits in the zone have been constructed efficiently. A number of these entrances and exits featuring strong capacity of check with intelligent facilities, including Beijing-Hong Kong-Macao Expressway Airport North Station, Shuanghe Lake Station and Shangqiu-Dengfeng Expressway Garden Expo Station, have been built and put into use one after another. Projects such as Yuanling Gucheng Station of Beijing-Hong Kong-Macao Expressway

达。京港澳高速公路、商登高速公路、安罗高速公路等多条高速公路以及 G107、G310 在此交汇，这些公路都能与新郑国际机场、郑州南站无缝衔接。目前，1000 千米的卡车航班范围基本覆盖了京津冀、长三角两大世界级城市群及关中城市群、环渤海经济圈等。

结合高速公路网络布局，近年来，航空港实验区境内的高速公路出入口建设一直在高效推进。包括京港澳高速航空港区北站、双鹤湖站以及商登高速园博园站等在内的一批通过能力强、设施智能的高速公路出入口陆续建设并投用。京港澳高速苑陵故城站等项目也在积极推进。将高速公路出入口与市政路网两者的规划建设有机结合，高速公路的运输作用将得到更大程度的发挥。

京港澳高速与商登高速在航空港实验区交汇
The Intersection of Beijing-Hong Kong-Macao Expressway and Shangqiu-Dengfeng Expressway in the Zhengzhou Airport Economy Zone

目前，航空港实验区"三纵两横"高速路网已经形成，"三纵四横"国省干线网络正加速完善，以高速公路、铁路、民航为主体的综合交通

are also being actively promoted. By organically combining the planning and construction of expressway entrances and exits with municipal road network, the transportation role of expressways will be brought into full play.

At present, the expressway network featuring three vertical and two horizontal lines in the zone has been formed. The network of trunk national and provincial expressways featuring three vertical and four horizontal lines is accelerating the improvement. The comprehensive transportation system with expressways, railways and civil aviation as the main parts supports to build a seamless multi-modal transportation system.

Nowadays, aviation and railway are vital to integrate regional economy and culture and to bring different parts of the world closer, while making speed economy popular. As the term suggests, speed economy is to rapidly meet various needs of customers for excess profits. John Kasarda, the founder of the theoretical model of aviation city, chief consultant of Zhengzhou Airport Economy Zone, and president of Aerotropolis Institute China, said that time was not only cost, but also money. By seamlessly connecting highways, railways and air transport, aviation metropolises help local, national and international enterprises reduce time costs and create speed economy.

位于新郑国际机场 T2 航站楼地下的城际铁路车站
Intercity Railway Station Located on the Underground of Terminal 2 of Xinzheng International Airport

体系，为构建"空、铁、陆"三网无缝联合的多式联运体系提供了重要支撑。

当今世界，航空运输、铁路运输已成为让区域经济与人文融入全球的重要通道，可以让世界各地快速拉近距离，"速度经济"这一概念也随之普及。速度经济，顾名思义是指企业因为快速满足顾客的各种需求，从而带来超额利润的经济。航空都市理论模型创立者、航空港实验区首席顾问、航都院院长约翰·卡萨达说，时间不仅仅是成本，更是金钱。通过无缝连接高速公路、铁路和空运，航空大都市帮助本土、全国性以及国际性企业降低时间成本，为这些企业创造了"速度经济"。

1978年秋天，当时正在日本考察的邓小平坐在新干线高铁列车上感慨"就感觉到快，有催人跑的意思"。今天，中国的发展跑出了令世人惊叹的"中国速度"，这种速度所带来的快捷与便利，以及所凝结的拼尽全力与时间赛跑的精神，正深刻影响着中国的发展，影响着人们的工作、学习和生活。

现在，越来越多家在郑州周边地区的年轻人选择来到航空港实验区就业，高铁、城铁、高速公路、快速路等组成的交通网络，可以让他们畅快往返于工作地和家乡，昔日"孔雀东南飞"的情况开始有所改变。随着大批在外高端人才向中原"流动"，越来越多的人正将自己的事业、生活与河南、与航空港实验区"结缘"。

发达的交通网络无疑大大降低了很多领域的经济、时间成本，相应的商务、会展、文化等方面也得以进一步发展。目前，航空港实验区"国际经济文化交流中心"正在完善规划、推进构建。对于政务商务来说，高铁能更加方便人才的交流，促进更多的人才向中心聚集，从而带动当地产业升级和社会经济发展。

"世界那么大，我想去看看"，从航空港实验区出发，人们乘高铁一小时可以通达河南省内任何地市，3个小时基本覆盖长三角、京津冀、山东半岛和西安、长沙、武汉等主要区域及城市，6个小时可覆盖主要

In the autumn of 1978, Deng Xiaoping, who was on an inspection tour in Japan at that time by Shinkansen, Japanese high-speed train, said with emotion, "I feel as fast as being urged to run." Today, China's development has run at the amazing China speed, which brings rapidness, convenience and the spirit of racing against time at our best, profoundly affecting China's development, as well as people's work, study and life.

Now, increasing number of young people nearby Zhengzhou choose to work in the Zhengzhou Airport Economy Zone. The transportation network composed of high-speed rails, intercity rails, highways and expressways can allow them to travel freely between workplace and home. The brain drain has been changed since then. With a large number of high-end talents flowing to the Central Plains, a growing number of people work and live in the zone and Henan.

The well-developed transportation network has undoubtedly greatly reduced the economic and time costs in many fields, while stimulating business, conference and exhibition and culture. At present, the International Economic and Cultural Exchange Center in the zone is improving its planning before speeding up the construction. For government affairs and business, high-speed train can facilitate the exchange of talents and bring more talents to the center, thus promoting local industrial upgrading and social and economic development.

As is said, the world is so big that I want to see it. Starting from the zone, people can go to any city in Henan by high-speed rail in one hour; in three hours basically to the Yangtze River Delta, Beijing-Tianjin-Hebei, Shandong Peninsula, as well as Xi'an, Changsha and Wuhan; in six hours to the coastal developed areas and Chengdu-Chongqing areas. This is undoubtedly a great benefit for people who want to experience the time-honored and diverse cultures of Henan and China. When getting off the plane from the Xinzheng International Airport, you can go to Xuchang for knowing the culture of the Three Kingdoms, to Kaifeng for visiting the Millennium City Park, and to Luoyang for enjoying peony by high-speed train or car within one hour. It is possible now to drink Hot Pepper Soup (spicy soup) in Henan in the morning, to eat pita bread soaked in lamb soup in Xi'an at noon and to enjoy the magnificent desert of Jiayuguan Pass at night.

When the Aerial Silk Road is linked with the star-shaped high-speed rail hub and the expressway network featuring three vertical and two horizontal lines,

从郑州南站引出的郑阜高铁、郑万高铁正线
Main lines of Zhengzhou-Fuyang High-speed Railway and Zhengzhou-Wanzhou High-speed Railway Starting from Zhengzhou South Railway Station

沿海发达地区和成渝地区。这对于想感受河南乃至全中国悠久而多样文化的人们无疑是一大福利,当你从新郑国际机场走下飞机,坐上高铁或汽车,想到许昌品位三国文化、到开封游览清明上河园、到洛阳欣赏牡丹,只需不到一小时。早上喝河南胡辣汤,中午吃西安羊肉泡馍,晚上领略嘉峪关壮美大漠的愿望,如今已经成为现实。

当"空中丝绸之路"与"贴地飞行"的"米"字形高铁枢纽、"三纵两横"高速公路网络联系在一起,经济加速腾飞、文化增进交融,生活自然也更加精彩,河南与全国乃至世界的"距离"从未如此之近。当你走遍河南省,走遍全中国,又回到航空港实验区,回到新郑国际机场,

these results are achieved: accelerating the economy, enhancing cultural exchanges, making life more fascinating, and bringing Henan that closer to China and the world. When you travel over Henan and China and go back to the zone and the airport, you will feel that the world is right in front of you again.

Located in the Central Plains, Henan reaches China and the world by the truck network covering more than 70 large- and medium-sized cities in China, and the radial high-speed train network, and the aviation network covering major economies in the world across Europe, America and Asia. Building a comprehensive transportation system featuring land-air docking, multi-modal transport, internal rapidity and external smoothness, lays a vital foundation for

"铁、公、机" 多式联运日渐成型
A Multimodal Transportation System with Railways, Expressways and Civil Aviation as the Main Parts Is Taking Shape

你将再次感受到，世界就在你眼前。

地处中原，辐射全国，横跨欧美亚三大经济区覆盖全球主要经济体的航线网络、覆盖全国70余座大中城市的卡车航班网络、郑州"米"字形高铁网络……构建"陆空对接、多式联运、内捷外畅"的综合交通体系，是让航空港实验区能够从无名航空小镇向国际航空大都市发展的重要基础。

在约翰·卡萨达看来，基于郑州在区域位置、交通枢纽上的先天优势，新郑国际机场具有非常高的竞争力。他还认为，"中国的航空大都市"品牌的打造，将扩大航空港实验区影响力，向全球展现航空都市发展建设的典范形象。

2019年，郑州入选国家发展改革委员会、交通运输部联合发布的国家物流枢纽建设名单，是入选名单中唯一的空港型国家物流枢纽。未来，航空港实验区将充分发挥"四路协同"的叠加优势，全力推进国际航空运输网、"米"字形高铁网和轨道交通网"三网"融合，加快形成以航空为主的国际交通、以高铁为主的国内交通、以城市轨道为主的大都市交通网络，促进国际陆港、综合保税区、国际空港和高铁物流基地的联动发展，打造"一带一路"和"空中丝绸之路"融合发展节点，建成"航空+高铁+城铁+地铁+普铁+快速路"高效衔接的国际综合交通枢纽。

developing the zone from an unknown aviation town to an international aviation metropolis.

In John Kasarda's view, the airport has very high competitiveness due to Zhengzhou's inherent advantages in regional location and transportation hub. He also believes that building the brand of China's Aerotropolis will make the zone be known by the world as a typical example of developing aviation metropolis.

In 2019, Zhengzhou was selected into the list of national logistics hub construction jointly issued by the National Development and Reform Commission and the Ministry of Transport, as the only airport hub. In the future, the Zhengzhou Airport Economy Zone will give full play to the advantages of superposition brought by four silk roads in the air and sea as well as on the land and internet, make every effort to integrate the networks of international aviation and rail transit, and star-shaped high-speed train network. The network with international aviation, domestic high-speed rail and metropolitan urban rail at its core, promotes the coordinated development of international land port and airport, comprehensive bonded zone, and high-speed rail logistics base, so as to build a development node of the Belt and Road and Aerial Silk Road, and an international comprehensive transportation hub with efficient connection among aviation, high-speed rail, city rail, subway, general-speed rail and expressway.

第二章

开放大门户

Chapter 2

Opening-up to the World

敞开胸襟，张开双臂，热切迎接高水平开放，不沿边、不靠海、不临江的河南，将"航空港""自贸区""跨境电商综试区""大数据综试区"等新平台、新载体、新动能、新要素统统纳入囊中，从内陆腹地一跃成为开放前沿。自获批以来，航空港实验区拥抱五洲四海，迎接八面来风，为我国内陆地区探索出一条扩大开放、转型发展的新路径，带动整个河南产业结构的调整升级，加速融入全球产业链条中，为高质量发展提供产业支撑和不竭动力。

一、口岸经济通世界

提起全民购物狂欢，人们的第一反应一定是"双十一"。

"双十一"起源于淘宝商城（天猫）在 2009 年 11 月 11 日举办的网络促销活动，自此成为购物狂欢节的固定日期。"买买买"风潮席卷国内外，销售额和订单量屡屡刷新纪录。2020 年"双十一"期间，全网实现销售额 5249 亿元，同比增长 28%，其中天猫实时物流订单量突破 22.5 亿单，约等于 2010 年全年中国快递量的总和。

这是网购狂欢的"盛宴"，也是电商物流的"大考"：面对巨大的流量压力和高频、高额、高密度的交易场景，如何为用户提供稳定而流畅的购物体验？航空港实验区交出了令人满意的答卷。

2020 年"双十一"深夜，郑州新郑综合保税区跨境电商保税物流中心保税仓内灯火通明。6600 余名员工有条不紊地登记信息、打包货品、扫码、贴单……一台又一台快递车辆的发动机声奏出激昂旋律，满载着消费者的期盼与惊喜奔向四方。

2020 年 11 月 1—11 日，航空港实验区跨境电商"双十一"促销活动合计申报单量 1151.05 万单，货值 13 亿元，同比去年分别增长 44.09%、42.88%。其中进口 775.29 万，货值 12.21 亿元，位居全国第二，仅次于宁波。11 月 11 日当天，进出口共申报 321.79 万单。

Opening its mind and opening its arms, Henan Province, which is not along the border, not by the sea, not by the river, is eagerly welcoming everyone. Henan is opening its doors wide and bringing all new platforms, new carriers, new driving forces and new elements, such as an airport, free trade zone, cross-border e-commerce comprehensive zone and big data comprehensive zone into its basket, aiming to leap from the inland hinterland to the forefront of opening up. Since its approval, the Zhengzhou Airport Economy Zone has embraced people from every corner of the world, explored a new path of expanding opening up and development mode transformation for inland areas of China, and promoted the adjustment and upgrading of the industrial structure of Henan as a whole. Henan has also accelerated its integration into the global industrial chain, and provided industrial support and inexhaustible motive force for high-quality development.

I. Port Economy Connecting with the World

When it comes to the national shopping spree, people's first reaction must be "Double Eleven".

"Double Eleven" originated from the online promotion held by Taobao Mall (Tmall) on November 11, 2009, and has since become a fixed date for a shopping carnival. The wave of "Buy! Buy! Buy!" swept across the country and abroad, with sales and orders setting new records. During the "Double Eleven" period in 2020, the sales of the whole network reached 524.9 billion *yuan*, up 28% year-on-year, among which Tmall's real-time logistics orders exceeded 2.25 billion, which was almost equal to the total express delivery volume in China in 2010.

This is the "feast" of online shopping carnival and also the "big test" to e-commerce logistics. Faced with huge shipment pressure and high-frequency, high-value and high-density trading scenarios, how can we provide users with a stable and smooth shopping experience? Zhengzhou Airport Economy Zone gave a satisfactory answer.

On the night of November 11 of 2020, the Cross-border E-commerce Bonded Logistic Center of Xinzheng Comprehensive Bonded Zone which is in the Zhengzhou Airport Economy Zone was a bright light. More than 6,600 employees were busy with registering information, packing goods, scanning

郑州新郑综合保税区保税物流中心，工人正在分拣货物
Workers in Bonded Logistics Center at Xinzheng Comprehensive Bonded Zone are sorting packages.

在国际贸易受到新冠肺炎疫情影响的情况下，这个位于我国中部的综合保税区跨境电商交易为何逆势上扬？

codes and posting bills ... The express trucks produced a passionate melody with their engines, which were full of consumers' expectations and joy while they were preparing to rush in all directions.

From November 1 to 11 of the year 2020, during "Double Eleven" promotional festival, in the Zhengzhou Airport Economy Zone the total declared entries of cross-border e-commerce were 11.5105 million, with a value of 1.3 billion *yuan*, up by 44.09% and 42.88% respectively, compared with last year. Among them, imports were 7,752,900, with a value of 1.221 billion *yuan*, ranking second in China and second only to Ningbo. On November 11, a total of 3,217,900 import and export declarations were made.

When international trade was affected by the novel coronavirus pneumonia epidemic, why did the cross-border e-commerce transactions in this comprehensive bonded zone, located in central China, rise against the trend?

Since 2020, the Zhengzhou Airport Economy Zone has adhered to the general principle of "stabilizing imports and promoting exports", taking the road of "hub + opening up", initiating the business model of "cross-border e-commerce + professional port" in cargo charter flights, launched special charter flights in Southeast Asia, such as "Zhengzhou-Kuala Lumpur" and "Zhengzhou-Bangkok" flights. The cargo planes traveled through with full cabins. These not only laid cross-border export channels, but also met the demand of inland areas for imported fruits, cold and fresh products, aquatic products, meat and other goods. The newly opened "Zhengzhou-Bangkok" cross-border export charter line, in 2020, has grown from the initial 2 flights per week to the current 4 flights per week.

Taking optimizing the business environment as a breakthrough, the Zhengzhou Airport Economy Zone has set up a cross-border e-commerce "service working group" in conjunction with customs, Henan Single Window and other departments, and has successively launched more than ten new measures, such as facilitating customs clearance, implementing "7 / 24" customs clearance, exploring cross-border businesses, including "9710 mode (applicable to goods directly exported by cross-border e-commerce)" and "9810 mode (applicable to goods exported from overseas warehouses by cross-border e-commerce)", over-the-counter drugs (OTC), 3C products and pet food, and continuously optimizing

2020年以来，航空港实验区坚持"稳进口、促出口"的总体思路，走"枢纽+开放"的路子，创新推出"跨境电商+专业口岸"货运包机业务模式，先后开辟"郑州—吉隆坡""郑州—曼谷"等东南亚专线包机，货机往返不空仓，既铺设了跨境出口通道，又满足了内陆地区对进口水果、冰鲜、水产、肉类等货物的需求。2020年新开通的"郑州—曼谷"跨境出口包机专线，从初始的每周2班已经发展到目前每周4班双来回。

以优化营商环境为突破口，航空港实验区联合海关、河南单一窗口等多部门成立跨境电商"服务工作组"，先后推出了十多项便利化通关等新举措，实行"7×24"通关，探索开展"9710"、"9810"、非处方药（OTC）、3C产品、宠物食品等跨境业务，不断优化业务流程，方便企业拓展品种。

河南罗布长风供应链管理有限公司自入驻郑州新郑综合保税区后，贸易额增长近5倍。北上广深的服装、鞋帽汇聚郑州，通过跨境包机出口，回程带回东南亚特色产品，之后分销全国。2020年上半年，该公司"郑州—吉隆坡"和"郑州—曼谷"的全货包机80余架次，进出口贸易额超过4000万美元，直接带动就业百余人。副总经理禹海叶赞叹地说："郑州地理位置优越，服务保障到位。"

国际航空运输网、"米"字形高铁网、高速公路网在这里融合，货物飞越大洋，紧接着是火车、货车的接力赛跑，是陆上交通运输的综合配套。无数与禹海叶一样的创业者穿梭其间，乘着越来越快捷的物流网，奔向充满希望的未来。

业内人士分析认为，航空港实验区具有的强大物流、政策等优势正不断显现，已经成为在国内具有相对竞争力和影响力的跨境电商发展基地和知名电商的汇集地，形成包括电商平台、仓储、物流、关务、结算企业在内的跨境产业链，产业集聚效应不断显现。

截至2020年底，在航空港实验区电子口岸平台备案的跨境电商企业共有804家，其中电商企业381家，平台企业315家，物流企业32家，

business processes to facilitate the development of new products.

Since Henan Luobu Changfeng Supply Chain Management Co., Ltd. settled in Zhengzhou Xinzheng Comprehensive Bonded Zone, its trade volume has increased nearly five times. Clothing, shoes and hats from Beijing, Shanghai, Guangzhou and Shenzhen are gathered in Zhengzhou, and are exported by cross-border charter flights. Southeast Asian specialty products are brought back on their return journey and then distributed throughout the country. In the first half of 2020, the company had more than 80 charter flights flying in Zhengzhou-Kuala Lumpur and Zhengzhou-Bangkok lines, and the import and export trade volume exceeded 40 million US dollars, providing about 100 job positions. Its deputy general manager, Yu Haiye, said heartfeltly, "Zhengzhou has a super good geographical position and proper service guarantee."

The international air transport network, the star-shaped high-speed rail network and the expressway network merge here in Zhengzhou, thus after the imported goods are landed from planes, they can be soon relayed by trains and trucks, which is a comprehensive supporting system for land transportation. Countless entrepreneurs, like Yu Haiye, travel by the networks, riding a faster and faster logistics network to a promising future.

According to experts, the advantages of strong logistics and policies in the Zhengzhou Airport Economy Zone are constantly emerging. Zhengzhou has become a cross-border e-commerce development base with relatively high competitiveness and influence in China. It has also become a gathering place for well-known e-commerce companies, forming a cross-border industrial chain, including e-commerce platforms, warehousing, logistics, customs and settlement enterprises. The industrial agglomeration effect is constantly emerging.

By the end of 2020, there were 804 cross-border e-commerce enterprises registered on the electronic port platform of the Zhengzhou Airport Economy Zone, including 381 e-commerce enterprises, 315 platform enterprises, 32 logistics enterprises, 38 customs declaration enterprises, 19 warehousing enterprises and 19 payment enterprises. Half of the top 10 well-known cross-border import e-commerce platforms in China have already entered the zone to establish bases and carried out their business, which include Taobao Global Purchase, Tmall International, Vipshop International, Jingdong International, Suning Overseas

报关企业 38 家、仓储企业 19 家、支付企业 19 家。全国排名前十的知名跨境进口电商平台中，有一半已经入区建立基地、开展业务，包括淘宝全球购、天猫国际、唯品国际、京东国际、苏宁海外购等；在国内外知名跨境出口电商平台中，阿里速卖通、eBay 等已实现入驻，中国邮政在这里设立分拨中心，已实现规模化、常态化运营，形成了相对完整的产业链。

阿里巴巴集团于 1999 年在中国杭州创立，是目前全球最大的网上及移动商务公司。早在几年前，阿里巴巴集团便开始向河南抛出"橄榄枝"——2013 年 11 月，河南省政府与菜鸟网络科技有限公司签署战略合作框架协议；2014 年 6 月，河南省政府与阿里巴巴集团签署云计算和大数据战略合作框架协议。

是什么让阿里巴巴频频"花落"河南？创始人马云说，河南消费潜力巨大，区位优势突出，"在郑州建设航空港是一个非常具有前瞻性的战略"，"相信双方通过现代物流和电子商务、云计算和大数据等领域的合作，能够激活和扩大跨境贸易，发挥郑州国际航空货运枢纽和国际陆港物流的优势，便利老百姓的衣食住行，带动社会公共服务的效率提升"。

未来，航空港实验区将把跨境电商打造成规模优势明显、产业优势突出、产业链完整的中部地区跨境产业基地。在产业结构上，进一步扩大航空物流型跨境电商出口比重，更好地带动河南全省的产业升级。

以跨境电商产业的快速发展为见证，一个种类多、功能全、效率高的立体大口岸体系正在航空港实验区快速形成，助推郑州加快成为国际物流枢纽。国家一类航空口岸新郑国际机场、中部地区第一个综合保税区郑州新郑综合保税区、肉类口岸、活牛口岸、邮政口岸、药品口岸、进境水果指定口岸、食用水生动物指定口岸等，为河南打通了进一步联结世界、融入全球的路径。

2013 年，航空港实验区获批之初，也正是郑州邦达天原供应链管

Purchase, etc. Among the well-known cross-border export e-commerce platforms at home and abroad, Ali Express and eBay have settled in. China Post has set up a distribution center here, which has realized large-scale and normal operation and formed a relatively complete industrial chain.

Alibaba Group, founded in 1999 in Hangzhou, China, is currently the world's largest online and mobile commerce company. A few years ago, Alibaba Group began to express its will of cooperation to Henan. In November 2013, Henan Provincial Government signed a strategic cooperation framework agreement with Cainiao Network Technology Co., Ltd. (a branch company of Alibaba). In June 2014, Henan Provincial Government and Alibaba Group signed a strategic cooperation framework agreement on cloud computing and big data.

What causes Alibaba to be so cooperative with Henan? Founder of Alibaba, Jack Ma once said, "Henan has great consumption potential, and outstanding location advantage. Building an Airport Economy Zone in Zhengzhou is a very forward-looking strategy. I believe that through cooperation in modern logistics and e-commerce, cloud computing and big data, the two sides can activate and expand cross-border trade, give full play to the advantages of Zhengzhou International Air Cargo Hub and land port logistics, thus facilitate people's food, clothing, housing and transportation, and promote the efficiency of social public services."

In the future, the Zhengzhou Airport Economy Zone will turn cross-border e-commerce into a cross-border industrial base in central China with obvious scale advantage, prominent industrial advantage and a complete industrial chain. In terms of industrial structure, the Zone will further expand its proportion of cross-border e-commerce exports, based on aviation logistics, to better promote the industrial upgrading of Henan Province.

Witnessed by the rapid development of cross-border e-commerce industry, a three-dimensional port system with many types of service, full functions and high efficiency is rapidly forming in the Zhengzhou Airport Economy Zone, boosting Zhengzhou to become an international logistics hub. Xinzheng International Airport, as a national first-class airport, plus the Xinzheng Comprehensive Bonded Zone, the first comprehensive bonded zone in central China: a meat port, live cattle port, postal port, drug port, designated port for imported fruits,

理有限公司总经理郭黎民创业之初,当时,他"隐约觉得机会要来了,但还不清楚具体方向在哪儿"。后来,一条又一条"重磅新闻"、一个又一个"利好消息",让他欢欣鼓舞,也看到了无限商机。航线通到哪儿,就把生意做到哪儿。如今,他的公司仅鲜花进口量,一年就有4万多千克。一架架满载玫瑰和郁金香的飞机,正让寻常的日子变得馥郁而多彩。

2019年9月25日15时30分,一批来自荷兰的鲜切花抵达新郑国际机场,一小时内就完成了通关手续,分拨至全国各地。"为吸引以鲜切花、水果为代表的更多大宗生鲜货物从郑州入境,郑州海关创新通关流程,实现了布控查验与现场检疫一次完成,在保证检疫有效性的同时,大幅压缩了通关时间。"郑州海关有关负责人介绍说。

近年来,挪威的三文鱼、孟加拉国的活黄鳝、荷兰的赤颈袋鼠等生鲜物品和大宗活体动物已经成为郑州航空口岸的"常客"。郑州海关为生鲜货物开辟绿色通道,实行"提前申报、简化流程、货到验放"的快速通关模式,配套采取"7×24小时"通关保障,建立智能卡口和整板交接平台,实现生鲜冷链货物智慧监管,其中对活体动物和大宗单一商品货物,允许实行"机坪理货、机坪验放",实现海关高效运作和企业通关成本日益降低的良性循环。

一个开放的时代,带来的是对人们生活方式的深刻改变。

在智利,距首都圣地亚哥50千米的纳提瓦车厘子种植园,种植面积达30公顷,车厘子年产量为150—200吨,其中95%出口到中国。

在荷兰,有百年历史的老牌花卉经销商西尔丰达公司,每周向郑州空运两批鲜花,每批重量为0.5—1吨。

十多个小时的飞行,跨过8000千米的距离,来自卢森堡本土的宝鼎啤酒抵达新郑国际机场。航空运输把"新鲜"概念发挥到了极致,啤酒从卢森堡生产出厂到进入中国市场,不超过三天时间。

西班牙Inditex集团的服装包机,每周都会沿着郑州—卢森堡货运航线飞来。这些时尚服饰在郑州完成清关后,很快被分拨至全国各大城

designated port for edible aquatic animals, etc. are jointly opening up a path for Henan to be further connected with the world and integrated into the world.

河南进口肉类指定口岸
Designated Port for Imported Meat in Henan

When the Zhengzhou Airport Economy Zone was granted, 2013 was also the year that Guo Limin, general manager of Zhengzhou Bangda Tianyuan Supply Chain Management Co., Ltd. had just started up his business. He said: "At that time, I vaguely felt that the opportunity is coming, but it is not clear where the specific direction is." Later, one after another "big news" and one after another "good news" made him rejoice and he saw great business opportunities. Wherever the airline leads, the business will be there. This is what Guo Limin did later. Today, his company imports more than 40,000 kilograms of flowers a year, and this is just one of his many businesses. Planes loaded with roses and tulips are making ordinary life rich and colorful.

At 15: 30 on September 25, 2019, a batch of fresh cut flowers from the Netherlands arrived at Xinzheng International Airport. After just one hour's customs clearance, the flowers were then soon distributed to all parts of the country. "In order to attract more bulk fresh goods, such as fresh cut flowers

市、进入商场……

全世界的优质商品源源流入,"进口货"变得触手可及。吃加拿大蓝莓,喝白俄罗斯牛奶,品德国啤酒,用澳大利亚保健品,赏荷兰郁金香……已成为不少中国内地居民的日常消费。一趟趟"跨洋之旅",正勾勒出一条"全球—郑州—全国"的贸易轨迹,折射着河南连天接地、买卖全球的澎湃活力。

2020年4月16日上午,河南省人民政府在航空港实验区举办中国邮政郑州航空邮件处理中心项目、新郑国际机场北货运区工程开工仪式,河南省委常委、常务副省长黄强出席开工仪式并宣布工程正式开工。

中国邮政郑州航空邮件处理中心项目是河南省人民政府与中国邮政战略合作的重要内容,是河南邮政口岸建设的重要组成部分,也是充分利用郑州区位交通优势和多式联运的航空物流优势,丰富完善邮政口岸功能的重要保障。

项目建成后,日均邮件处理量可达68.6万件,将有力支撑航空港实验区建成具有区域影响力的现代物流产业基地,有力推动郑州打造成全国国际邮件枢纽口岸,对于助力打通"大动脉"、畅通"微循环",提高河南"空中丝绸之路"辐射能力,加快打造内陆开放高地都具有十分重大的现实和长远意义。

紧紧围绕"空中丝绸之路"建设,加快"枢纽+口岸+保税+产业基地"融合集聚,航空港实验区走出了一条富有特色的临空经济发展之路,外贸进出口连续6年占据河南省半壁江山,临空经济发展走在全国前列。2020年,航空港实验区实现经济社会逆势增长,外贸进出口总额突破4000亿元,增长18.5%,达4447亿元,全省外贸占比持续保持60%以上。全年共完成跨境电商进出口业务1.39亿单、货值达113.9亿元,同比分别增长91.72%、62.01%,跨境电商单量从2015年的74.6万单迅速上升到2020年的13933.81万单,业务量占郑州跨境综试区总量的比重从1.59%增至60.62%,连续5年实现翻番式增长,已成为郑州

and fruits, to be imported through Zhengzhou Airport, Zhengzhou Customs innovated the clearance process, realized the completion of control inspection and on-site quarantine at one time, which greatly reduced the customs clearance time while ensuring the effectiveness of quarantine", a director in Zhengzhou Customs said.

In recent years, Norwegian salmon, Bangladesh's live ricefield eel, Hollands red-necked kangaroo and other fresh items and a large number of live animals have become "frequent visitors" to Zhengzhou Airport. Zhengzhou Customs opens up a green channel for fresh goods, implementing the fast customs clearance mode of "declaring in advance, simplifying the process, inspecting and releasing ASAP". It also supports the "7 / 24" customs clearance guarantee, establishes a smart card port and a whole board handover platform, and realizes intelligent supervision of fresh cold chain goods, in which "apron tally and apron inspection and release" are allowed for live animals and single bulk commodity goods. By all these measures, a virtuous circle of efficient customs operation and low-cost customs clearance for enterprises is achieved.

An open era will surely bring about profound changes in people's lifestyles.

In Chile, the Nativa Cherry Plantation, covering an area of 30 hectares, is 50 kilometers away from the capital Santiago, whose annual output is 150 to 200 tons of cherries, 95% of which are exported to China.

In Netherlands, Hilverda De Boer, a century-old flower distributor, airlifts two batches of flowers to Zhengzhou every week, each batch weighing 0.5 to 1 ton.

After more than ten hours of air travel, over a distance of 8,000 kilometers, Baofferding beer from Luxembourg can arrive at Xinzheng International Airport. Air transport has brought the concept of "freshness" into full play. It takes a can of the beer no more than three days to enter the Chinese market soon after it leaves its Luxembourg-based production line.

The clothing charter flights of Spain's Inditex Group travel along the Zhengzhou-Luxembourg freight route every week. After completing customs clearance in Zhengzhou, these fashionable clothes are quickly distributed to major cities across the country and shopping malls...

High-quality goods from all around the world keep flowing in, putting

琳琅满目的进口货品
A Dazzling Array of Imported Goods

"the imported goods" within reach of Zhengzhou. Eating Canadian blueberries, drinking Belarusian milk, tasting German beer, using Australian health care products and enjoying Dutch tulips have become the daily consumption habit of many mainland Chinese residents. The "cross-ocean trips" are outlining a trace track of "world-Zhengzhou-China", reflecting the surging vitality of Henan by buying and selling around the world.

On the morning of April 16, 2020, Henan Provincial People's Government held the commencement ceremony of China Post Zhengzhou Air Mail Processing Center Project and Xinzheng International Airport North Cargo Area Project in the Zhengzhou Airport Economy Zone. Huang Qiang, member of the Standing Committee of Henan Provincial Party Committee and executive vice governor, attended the commencement ceremony and announced the official start-up of the project.

China Post Zhengzhou Air Mail Processing Center Project is an important part of the strategic cooperation between Henan Provincial People's Government and China Post, an important part of Henan Post Port Construction, and an important guarantee for making full use of Zhengzhou's regional transportation advantages and multimodal transport aviation logistics advantages to enrich and improve the functions of postal ports.

After the completion of the project, the daily average mail processing capacity can reach 686,000 pieces. It will strongly facilitate the Zhengzhou Airport Economy Zone in building into a modern logistics industry base with regional influence, vigorously promoting Zhengzhou to become a national international mail hub. It will also be of long-term significance for helping to open up the "aorta", smoothing the "microcirculation", improving the radiation capacity of Henan's "Aerial Silk Road" and accelerating the building of inland open-up highland.

Closely focusing on the construction of the "Aerial Silk Road" and accelerating the integration and agglomeration of "hub + port + bonded + industrial base", the Zhengzhou Airport Economy Zone has embarked on a distinctive road of airport economic development, with foreign trade import and export taking up half of Henan's total economy output for six consecutive years. Airport economic development in Henan is at the forefront of the country. In

跨境综试区最为强劲的业务增长点。

　　作为衡量地区对外经济"热度"的关键指标,这样的数字代表了在河南,一个对外开放的新高地正在形成。航空港实验区的区域竞争力不断提升,对郑州国家中心城市建设、中原更加出彩的"龙头""引领"作用不断增强。不同类型口岸的设立,犹如代表着开放与机遇的"风口",引来人流、物流、资金流、信息流在此汇聚,一张由各类企业集聚而成的产业大网开始在这里织就。

2020, the Zhengzhou Airport Economy Zone achieved economic and social contrarian growth, with the total import and export volume exceeding 400 billion *yuan*, an increase of 18.5% to 444.7 billion *yuan*, and the province's foreign trade accounted for more than 60% of the provincial total output. In the whole year, a total of 139 million cross-border e-commerce import and export business was completed, with a value of 11.39 billion *yuan*, up 91.72% and 62.01% respectively year-on-year. The number of cross-border e-commerce orders increased rapidly from 746,000 orders in 2015 to 139.3381 million orders in 2020. The proportion of business volume in the total cross-border comprehensive test area in Zhengzhou increased from 1.59% to 60.62%, achieving double growth for five consecutive years, becoming the strongest business growth point in the area.

As a key indicator to measure the "heat" of regional foreign economy, such figures symbolize a new highland of opening to the world is taking shape in Henan. The regional competitiveness of the Zhengzhou Airport Economy Zone has been continuously improved, and its leading role in the construction of Zhengzhou as a national central city and a more brilliant Central Plains has been continuously enhanced. The establishment of different types of ports is like a "window" representing openness and opportunities, attracting people flow, logistics, capital flow and information flow to gather here. An industrial network formed by various enterprises has begun to be woven here.

二、一颗种子结硕果

河南自古被称为"中原粮仓",是中国第一粮食加工大省、第一肉制品大省,农产品出口遍及全球 137 个国家和地区。但这里的特产不仅是小麦、玉米,"代工巨无霸"富士康科技集团(简称"富士康")的到来,为这个产粮大省引入"一颗苹果"。

作为河南现代制造业的核心集聚区之一,航空港实验区聚集了上千家企业,其中以富士康为代表的电子信息产业表现抢眼,每年带动全区贡献全省 60% 以上的进出口额。可以说,"没有富士康,就没有综保区,没有综保区,就没有郑州航空港"。

航空港实验区富士康科技园航拍
Aerial Photography of Foxconn Science and Technology Park in the Zhengzhou Airport Economy Zone

身处传统农耕大省,河南人做事讲求天时、地利、人和。庄稼要丰收,三者缺一不可。就电子信息产业而言,富士康在航空港实验区落地萌发、开枝散叶,也正是遵循了这一定律。

20 世纪 70 年代末,改革开放风起大潮涌。中国沿海地区最先凭借

II. From Seed to Fruits

Henan has been called "the granary of the Central Plains" since ancient times. It is China's largest grain processing province and the largest meat product province. Its agricultural products are exported to 137 countries and regions around the world. However, the specialties here are not only wheat and corn. The arrival of Foxconn Technology Group (hereinafter referred to as "Foxconn"), the "OEM Big Mac", has also introduced "an apple" to this major grain-producing province.

As one of the core gathering areas of Henan's modern manufacturing industry, the Zhengzhou Airport Economy Zone has gathered thousands of enterprises, of which the electronic information industry, represented by Foxconn, has performed well, driving the whole region to contribute more than 60% of the province's import and export volume every year. It can be said that "without Foxconn, there would be no Comprehensive Bonded Zone, furthermore, without the Comprehensive Bonded Zone, there would be no the Zhengzhou Airport Economy Zone".

Being in a traditional farming province, Henan people value the principle: things must be done at the right time, the right place, and with the right people. If a peasant wants a bumper harvest, all the three are indispensable. As far as the electronic information industry is concerned, Foxconn has followed this principle when it sprouted and spread its branches and leaves in the Zhengzhou Airport Economy Zone .

At the end of 1970s, the reform and opening-up began its surging. China's coastal areas were the first to make use of the east wind of opening-up, thus soon making its people rich and its economy strong. With the deepening of the reform, coastal areas began to change the mode of economic development by accelerating the transformation to a capital-technology-intensive and innovation-driven economy, and labor-intensive industries gradually turned to inland provinces. This was a rare opportunity for Henan to develop. Therefore, Henan's decision-makers acted quickly. They determined to "gather all forces and mobilize all positive factors", to get rid of the stereotype image of being "backward", "poor" and "weak".

开放的东风，迅速集聚资源，让人民富起来，经济强起来。随着改革的深入推进，沿海地区开始转变经济发展方式，加速向资金技术密集型、创新驱动型经济转变，劳动密集型等产业逐步转向内陆。这对于河南来说，是一次难得的发展机遇。于是，河南决策层迅速行动，决心"汇聚一切力量，调动一切积极因素"，甩掉"土""穷""弱"的帽子，方法就是——出台大招商经济刺激计划，吸引发达地区制造业等产业转移，促使传统农业大省向现代工业强省的转型升级。

2010年2月，河南省下发《河南省招商引资行动计划》。省政府连续召开4次全省招商引资工作会议，提出依托175个产业集聚区，充分发挥其筑巢引凤功能，高水平策划集聚区招商概念，按照"大项目—产业链—产业集群"的思路，以"区中园"建设为切入点，引导产业关联度大、成长性好的项目向产业集聚区集中，积极承接发达地区链式和集群式产业转移，促使招商引资、项目建设、产业发展同步推进。

"大招商"一时成为河南全省各地政府部门工作的重点，省会郑州更是连创开展活动最多、接待客商最多、签约项目最多、招商力度最大等数个全省之"最"。

转型之风入中原，上下同心谋发展，这是大势所趋，此为"天时"。

对于自身拥有的招商优势，河南人是清醒的。正如河南省某高层领导在招商推介中所说："以郑州为中心，画一个直径200千米的圆，其所辐射的人口和承载的城市，是世界任何地点都无法相比的，具有其他地方不具备的聚集和扩散效应。"

的确，相较于其他区域，河南及周边平原地区广阔，交通基础条件优越，发达的公路、铁路网络可快速通达京津冀、长三角、珠三角和成渝城市带，位于承接产业西移的第一梯队。交通物流成本和航空港的发展，直接拉大企业销售半径，为企业带来市场便利。河南丰富的劳动力资源和庞大的本地市场，也成为吸引沿海制造业企业落地的重要因素。

得天独厚的地理区位优势，可谓"地利"。

The method was to introduce a large-scale investment economic stimulus plan to attract the transfer of manufacturing industries in developed regions, and promote the transformation and upgrading of a traditional agricultural province to a modern industrial province.

In February 2010, Henan Province issued *The Action Plan for Attracting Investment to Henan Province*. The provincial government held four provincial investment promotion conferences. It proposed to rely on its 175 industrial clusters to play its full role in building nests to attract phoenixes. The concept of investment promotion in agglomeration areas was planned at a high level. Based on the idea of "big projects-industrial chains-industrial clusters" and taking the construction of "parks in the districts" as the breakthrough point, projects with large industrial relevance and good growth were guided to concentrate in industrial agglomeration areas. Chain and cluster industrial transfer in developed areas was actively undertaken to promote investment in the airport zone. Project construction and industrial development were soon conducted simultaneously.

During that period, "the large-scale investment economic stimulus plan" has become the focus of the work of government departments all over Henan Province. Zhengzhou, as the provincial capital, became the top city of the province in the following aspects: holding the most investment promotion conferences, hosting the largest number of investors and merchants, signing the most project contracts and offering the strongest investment incentives.

It was then in Henan the general trend for the transformation of enterprises, and all the people were devoted to promoting development. This is called the "right time".

Henan people are sober about their own advantages in attracting investment. Just as a senior leader of the Henan Provincial Government said in one of the investment promotion conferences, "Taking Zhengzhou as the center, if we draw a circle with a diameter of 200 kilometers, it will radiate a large population and a number of cities with which no others can compare in the world, and it has the agglomeration and diffusion effect that no other place can match."

Indeed, compared with other regions, Henan and its surrounding plain areas are vast and have superior transportation infrastructure. The developed road and railway networks can quickly reach Beijing-Tianjin-Hebei, Yangtze River Delta

富士康这只"巨凤",就是在这样"天时""地利"的背景下,挥师北迁、落栖中原的。但"天时""地利"只是一方面,更重要的还要"尽人事"。

早在2007年,郑州市政府就成立了"富士康科技集团郑州投资项目协调推进小组"。彼时,富士康内迁初成趋势,天津、武汉、廊坊等曾经与富士康有过合作的地方,纷纷向富士康抛出"橄榄枝",希望争取更多投资,这给河南的招商谈判工作组增加了不少的困难。河南省政府主要领导多次在内部会议上表示,现在一些大项目、好项目,往往多家、多市、多省在争,越是大项目、好项目,业主投资越谨慎,往往提出各种条件,这就有一个决断的问题,所以要在做好大量前提工作的基础上,必要时主帅出征,果断决策。

2010年,河南省委、省政府从全面实施中原经济区发展战略的大局出发,以建设航空经济枢纽为支点,把与富士康的合作作为全省承接产业转移的重中之重来抓。时任省长郭庚茂亲自参与谈判,协调解决重大问题。这一举动无疑打动了富士康团队,双方在一个月的时间内"秘密"进行了四轮商务谈判,谈判规模之大、参与范围之广、涉及领域之多均史无前例。

2010年6月20日,富士康董事长郭台铭首次来到郑州,郭庚茂亲临机场迎接会见。此行之后,双方草签《战略合作框架协议》,初步约定在电子信息产业、人力资源、物流、销售等领域展开合作,富士康投资河南的悬念终成定局。按照协议,富士康将在郑州建设一座超大型工业园,用作公司核心业务——苹果手机整机生产基地,园区规划占地面积达10平方千米、计划用工30万人。

为实现"七月签约、八月开工"的目标,郑州市成立了专项工作组,制定清晰简略的工作时间表,兵分两路投入富士康项目建设中。一路在郑州出口加工区,改造升级郑州出口加工区的7栋共计6.25万平方米的标准化厂房;另一路重点协助富士康方面完成相关工商注册、物流管

cities, Pearl River Delta cities and Chengdu-Chongqing urban belts, ranking the first echelon to undertake the westward movement of industries. The cost increase of transportation and logistics, the development of airports can directly widen the sales radius of enterprises and bring market convenience to enterprises. Henan's abundant labor resources and huge local market are also important factors in attracting coastal manufacturing enterprises to settle in.

The unique geographical advantage can be described as "the right place".

Foxconn, the "giant phoenix", moved northward and settled in the Central Plains under the background of "the right time" and "the right place". However, "the right time" and "the right place" are only one aspect, more importantly, it is the people's effort that is the critical factor.

As early as 2007, Zhengzhou Municipal Government established "Zhengzhou investment project coordination and promotion group for Foxconn project". At that time, Foxconn's migration to inland provinces was becoming a trend. Tianjin, Wuhan, Langfang and other places that had cooperated with Foxconn all expressed strong wills of cooperation to Foxconn in the hope of winning more investment. This added a lot of difficulties to Henan's investment negotiation group. The major leaders of Henan's provincial government emphasized many times at internal meetings, "Some big projects and good projects are now being contested by many cities and provinces. The bigger or the better the projects, are the more cautious the owners are in investing and often the more they demand. This is a question of decision. Therefore, on the basis of doing a lot of prerequisite work, the top leader should go out and make decisive decisions when necessary."

In 2010, seeking the overall situation of fully implementing the development strategy of the Central Plains Economic Zone, the Henan Provincial Party Committee and the Henan Provincial Government decided to take on the construction of an aviation economic hub as the fulcrum, to take the cooperation with Foxconn as the top priority for the province to undertake industrial transfer. Guo Gengmao, then governor, participated in person in the negotiations, coordinated departments and solved many major problems. This undoubtedly moved the Foxconn team. The two sides "secretly" held four rounds of business negotiations within one month. The scale of the negotiations, the scope of participation and the number of fields involved were unprecedented.

理、报关系统等配套手续。

7月3日,富士康一期项目厂房改造工程动工。项目建设各工地24小时施工不停歇,工作人员吃住在单位,轮歇上岗,从厂房改造开工到设备进场交接,仅用了15天。

7月23日,富士康旗下鸿富锦精密电子(郑州)有限公司在郑州市工商局注册成立,主要负责苹果手机整机生产项目。

8月2日,经过十几天的生产设备安装调试,富士康河南项目首条生产线在郑州出口加工区正式投产。

一个月的时间,一个面积达6万平方米、可容纳8000人作业的厂房改造完成,这让郭台铭感到"不可思议",竖起大拇指为"郑州速度"点赞:"通过富士康项目,可以自豪地说,别的省份能做到的,河南也能做到。"富士康副总经理林政辉也在多个场合称赞,在富士康集团的历史上,"郑州速度"不敢说"绝后",但肯定是空前的。

富士康员工上下班人潮

Foxconn Employees at Rush Hour

On June 20, 2010, Foxconn Chairman Guo Taiming flew to Zhengzhou for the first time. Guo Gengmao greeted him at the airport. After the meeting, the two sides signed *The Strategic Cooperation Framework Agreement*, basically agreeing to cooperate in the fields of electronic information industry, human resources, logistics and sales. The suspense of Foxconn's investment in Henan is a foregone conclusion. According to the agreement, Foxconn would build a super-large industrial park in Zhengzhou, which would be used as the core business of the company—Apple mobile phone production base. The park is to cover an area of 10 square kilometers and to provide jobs for 300,000 people.

In order to achieve the goal of "signing a contract in July and starting the production in August", Zhengzhou had set up a special working group to make out a clear and brief work schedule. The two groups began to conduct the construction project respectively at the same time. One team worked in Zhengzhou Export Processing Zone by renovating and upgrading 7 standardized factories with a total area of 62,500 square meters in Zhengzhou Export Processing Zone. The other team focused on assisting Foxconn to complete relevant industrial and commercial registration, logistics management, the customs declaration system and other supporting procedures.

On July 3, the factory building renovation project of Foxconn Phase I Project started. The construction of each project worked non-stop, 24 hours a day. The staff ate and lived in the construction sites, taking turns on their posts. It took only 15 days from the start of the factory building, renovation to the handover of factory plants.

On July 23, Foxconn's Hongfujin Precision Electronics (Zhengzhou) Co., Ltd. was registered and established in Zhengzhou Industrial and Commercial Bureau, which is mainly involved in the production project of Apple mobile phone.

On August 2, after more than ten days of installation and commissioning of production equipment, the first production line of Foxconn Henan Project was officially put into production in Zhengzhou Export Processing Zone.

In one month, the renovation of a factory building with an area of 60,000 square meters and a capacity of 8,000 people was completed, which made Guo Taiming feel "incredible" and gave a thumbs up to praise "Zhengzhou Speed", "Through the construction of Foxconn project in Henan, we can proudly say that

9月16日，富士康郑州科技园破土奠基，项目一期厂房建设面积140万平方米，到2011年底可实现超过14万人入驻。这一项目也标志着富士康真正的"产业大挪移"的开始。

10月24日，好消息再度传来，郑州新郑综合保税区获国务院批准设立，河南经济从此拥有了与世界接轨的平台，富士康则成为综合保税区第一家入驻企业。

2011年，为了对接服务富士康，郑州市成立了"五五办"工作小组，要求做到"五个一"，即一个项目、一个团队、一个方案、一条龙服务、一盯到底。作为回报，富士康董事长郭台铭也制定了一个"五五专案"，即五年内在河南创造5000亿元产值。

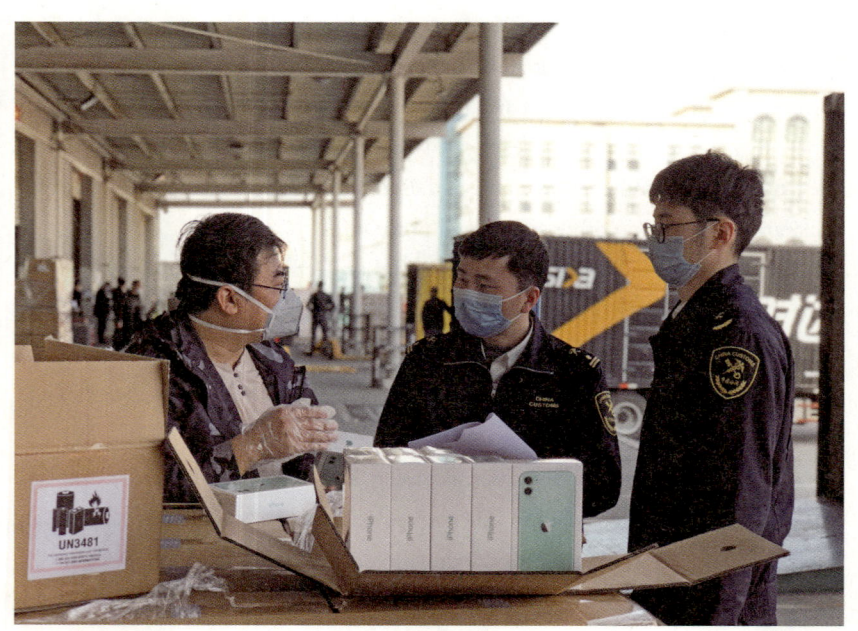

海关查验即将装机的苹果手机

Ready-to-be-loaded iPhones Inspected at Customs

数据显示，2011年，河南省进出口总值达326.4亿美元，较上年大幅增长83.1%，其中有52.6个百分点是由富士康拉动的。落地十年，富

what other provinces can do, Henan can also do it." Lin Zhenghui, deputy general manager of Foxconn, also praised on many occasions, "In the history of Foxconn Group, 'Zhengzhou Speed' may not forever be the fastest, but it is definitely unprecedented."

On September 16, Foxconn Zhengzhou Science and Technology Park broke ground and laid the foundation stone. The first phase of the project covers an area of 1.4 million square meters. By the end of 2011, more than 140,000 people were planned to settle in. This project also marks the beginning of Foxconn's real "industrial shift".

富士康郑州园区项目奠基仪式
Foundation-laying Ceremony of Foxconn Project in Zhengzhou

On October 24, good news came again. Zhengzhou Xinzheng Comprehensive Bonded Zone was approved by the State Council. Henan's economy boasted a platform to connect with the world. Foxconn has become the first enterprise to enter the Comprehensive Bonded Zone.

In 2011, in order to serve Foxconn, Zhengzhou set up a "Five-five Office" working group, promising "Five Ones", that is, one project, one team, one plan, one-stop service and one team sticking to the end. In return, Foxconn's Chairman Gou Taiming also formulated a "Five-five Plan", that is, to create an output value

士康苹果手机产量从零到近亿部,用令人惊叹的"郑州速度",打造出全球最大的苹果手机生产基地和富士康大陆地区单体规模最大的生产基地,年均产值 3000 亿元,超额完成"五五专案"。

如果把富士康看成是航空港实验区智能终端产业体系的"启动器",纷至沓来的招商引资项目则俨然组成了一台"产业发动机"。除富士康体系外,一些行业尖端企业开始在这里集聚,"头雁效应"开始显现。河南更是不敢懈怠,在成为全球重要的智能手机生产基地后,便开始拥抱更大的目标,整合全球电子产品供应链,打造国际电子信息产业基地。

2013 年 7 月 10 日,航空港实验区党工委、管委会正式揭牌。当天,首批落户的智能手机、液晶电视、现代物流等重点项目集中开工,总投资 166 亿元,拉开了以航空经济为引领的现代产业基地建设的序幕。而依据河南省委、省政府和郑州市委、市政府重点发展智能终端(手机)产业的战略决策,航空港实验区规划了 30 平方千米的智能手机产业制造基地。

航空港实验区智能终端(手机)产业园
Intelligent Terminal (Mobile Phone) Industrial Park in the Zhengzhou Airport Economy Zone

of 500 billion *yuan* in Henan within five years.

Data shows that in 2011, the total import and export value of Henan Province reached US $32.64 billion, a substantial increase of 83.1% over the previous year, of which 52.6% were driven by Foxconn. Ten years after landing, Foxconn's output of Apple mobile phones has gone from zero to nearly 100 million. Under the amazing "Zhengzhou speed", Foxconn has built the world's largest production base of Apple mobile phones and the largest single production base in mainland, with an average annual output value of 300 billion *yuan*. This achievement has greatly exceeded the "Five-five Plan".

If Foxconn is regarded as the "starter" of the intelligent terminal industry system in the Zhengzhou Airport Economy Zone , the following numerous investment promotion and capital introduction projects have become an "industrial engine". In addition to Foxconn system, some cutting-edge enterprises in their industries began to gather here, and the "Head Goose Effect" began to take place. Henan did not stop there. After becoming an important smart phone production base in the world, it began to embrace bigger goals, aiming to integrate the global electronic product supply chain and build an international electronic information industry base.

On July 10, 2013, the Party Committee and the Administrative Committee of the Zhengzhou Airport Economy Zone were officially established. On the same day, the first batch of key projects such as smart phones, LCD TVs and modern logistics started with a total investment of 16.6 billion *yuan*, which kicked off the construction of modern industrial bases focusing on aviation economy. According to the strategic decision of Henan Provincial Party Committee, Provincial Government and Zhengzhou Municipal Party Committee and Municipal Government to focus on the development of smart terminal (mobile phone) industry, the Zhengzhou Airport Economy Zone planned a 30-square-kilometer smart phone industry manufacturing base.

The Intelligent Terminal (Mobile Phone) Industrial Park in the Zhengzhou Airport Economy Zone, located in the southern high-end manufacturing cluster area, opened on January 13, 2014. The first phase of the initial area is 120,000 square meters. Twelve standardized factory buildings were put into use. The second phase of construction is 180,000 square meters. Eight factory buildings and

2014年1月13日，位于南部高端制造业集聚区的航空港实验区智能终端（手机）产业园开园。起步区一期12万平方米、12栋标准化厂房投入使用，二期18万平方米、8栋厂房、2栋配套于9月建成并投入使用。经过简单装修，上海中兴、深圳创维等12家手机制造企业首批入驻。根据规划，园区还将建造企业总部、手机研发、手机生产、配套产业、生活服务等功能区，规划重点围绕智能终端产品，积极引进包括品牌商、代工商、配套商、物流商、运营商在内的高端企业，建设融手机研发、产品设计、软件开发、整机制造、配件生产到销售、物流、售后于一体的全产业链模式。

在富士康郑州科技园、智能终端（手机）产业园的带动下，到2016年，航空港实验区手机产量已达到2.58亿部，约占全球手机产量的七分之一，成为名副其实的全球智能终端（手机）制造基地。这2.58亿部手机中，苹果手机1.26亿部，其他手机1.32亿部，"非苹果"手机产量首次超越苹果手机，智能终端企业一企独大的态势快速改变。

2016年9月28日，由航空港实验区国资平台兴港投资集团和民资企业田川实业合资运营的智能终端（手机）产业园B、C、D、E区开建。在先期形成的手机制造产业集群基础上，B、C区主推智能终端产品和软件的研发、设计与销售，建设全产业链模式；D、E区着力打造光电显示产业集群，涵盖玻璃基板、面板、模组、液晶显示器等领域，覆盖光电显示产业上、中、下游。

注册资本2亿元、专注光学和触控显示的高科技生产企业郑州联创电子有限公司，是上市公司联创电子科技股份有限公司的全资子公司。起初，这家上游公司只做镜头、镜片等核心零部件，2019年入驻智能终端（手机）产业园后，越来越多的客户看中其核心技术，指定要用联创产品。"市面上很多整机厂商都是购买零部件再进行组装，既然一部手机既要用到我们的镜头、又要用到我们的显示模块，不如'砍掉'中间商，直接和终端客户谈。"就这样，总经理廖细平开始带着团队布局整

two supporting buildings were completed and put into use in September. After simple decoration, twelve mobile phone manufacturers such as ZTE Corporation (Zhongxing Telecommunication Equipment) and Skyworth Group Co., Ltd. were among the first batch to settle in the new industrial park. According to the plan, the park would also build functional areas for corporate headquarters and for mobile phone research and development, mobile phone production, as well as for supporting industries and living services. The plan focused on intelligent terminal products and actively introduced high-end enterprises including brand vendors, agent vendors, matching dealers, logistics providers and operators, and was to ultimately build a full industrial chain model integrating mobile phone research

航空港实验区智能终端（手机）产业园鸟瞰图
An Aerial View of the Intelligent Terminal (Mobile Phone) Industrial Park in the Zhengzhou Airport Economy Zone

机产线。在航空港实验区管委会、商务和物流业发展局和园区运营中心的帮助下，郑州联创电子有限公司突飞猛进，一年间员工从100人壮大到2200人，实现手机整机月产能350万台，影像模组每月出货量1000万个，月均销售额1.5亿元，产品销往三星、小米、OPPO、vivo、传音、特斯拉等终端品牌厂商。

自2010年富士康智能手机项目落地以来，航空港实验区抢抓产业转移机遇，走出了一条以智能终端为突破口的电子信息产业转型发展的路子，现已有富士康、联创电子、宝聚丰等100余家智能终端企业入驻，

已落成的园区企业家俱乐部集酒店、报告厅、会客厅、健身房于一体
The Completed Entrepreneur Club in the Park Integrating a Hotel, a Lecture Hall, a Reception Hall and a Gym

and development, product design, software development, machine manufacturing, accessory production along with sales, logistics and post-sale services.

Driven by Foxconn Zhengzhou Science and Technology Park and the Intelligent Terminal (Mobile Phone) Industrial Park, by 2016, the output of mobile phones in the Zhengzhou Airport Economy Zone had reached 258 million, accounting for about one seventh of the global output of mobile phones, which made it a veritable global intelligent terminal manufacturing base. Among the 258 million mobile phones produced, there were 126 million iPhones and 132 million other mobile phones. For the first time, the output of other mobile phones surpassed that of iPhones, and the dominant situation of Foxconn among intelligent terminal enterprises changed rapidly.

The construction of B, C, D, E districts of the Intelligent Terminal (mobile phone) Industrial Park started on September 28, 2016.These districts are jointly operated by Xinggang Investment Group which is a state-owned platform of the Zhengzhou Airport Economy Zone, and Tianchuan Industry, a private enterprise. On the basis of the mobile phone manufacturing industry cluster formed in advance, the B and C districts mainly promote the research, development, design and sales of intelligent terminal products and software, and builds a whole industrial chain model. The D and E districts strive to build a photoelectric display industry cluster, covering the fields of glass substrates, panels, modules, liquid crystal displays, which includes the upper, middle and lower reaches of the photoelectric display industry.

Zhengzhou Lianchuang Electronics Co., Ltd. is a high-tech manufacturer with a registered capital of two hundred million *yuan* that focuses on optical and touch displays. It is a wholly-owned subsidiary of Lianchuang Electronics Technology Co., Ltd., a listed company. Initially, this upstream company only made core components such as camera lenses. After entering the Intelligent Terminal (mobile phone) Industrial Park in 2019, more and more customers took a fancy to its core technologies and chose to use Lianchuang's products. "Many complete machine manufacturers in the market buy parts and then assemble them. Since a mobile phone needs both our lenses and our display modules, it is better to cut out the middlemen and talk directly with end customers." In this way, Liao Xiping, the general manager, began to lead the team to lay out

实现了"从一颗苹果向一片果园"的快速突破。2019年，航空港实验区内智能终端及其配套企业进出口达到3464.06亿元人民币，占全区进出口总额的96.56%。从2011年到2019年，全区累计手机出货量超过15亿部，河南也因此成为中国境内仅次于广东的手机生产大省。

"水到则渠成。"航空港实验区商务和物流业发展局局长王飞这样评价眼前的变化，"航空港实验区智能终端产业正逐步由轻资产运营的整机组装，向重资产投入的新型显示、摄像模组等深加工领域拓展，向产业链上游的芯片、面板、研发设计、高端制造方面延伸，也向智能网联、智能家居、智慧医疗等应用产业链扩散。"

每一轮技术变革都孕育着重大发展机遇，抓得住、用得好，就可以实现产业的跨越甚至赶超。20世纪七八十年代，日本凭借发展大规模集成电路，在电子信息产业上大幅拉近与美国的距离；21世纪初，韩国、中国台湾抓住"显示革命"的机遇，通过大力发展TFT-LCD，在显示器件领域迅速崛起。而今，新一轮科技革命在全球范围内的勃兴，为发展中国家经济结构调整和新旧动能转换带来"弯道超车"的契机。

如何叠加劳动力与资本、技术和市场等优势，持续整合跨行业、跨区域、跨国界的各类要素资源，为产业链供应链注入"黏合剂"，助推制造业拾级而上？这是新形势下航空港实验区参与全球产业链供应链竞争和合作必须回答的命题。

2018年，航空港实验区进一步提出，要狠抓以智能终端为代表的世界级电子信息先进制造业集群培育，确立了"1+1+N"的发展理念。第一个"1"是富士康产业集群，第2个"1"是以智能终端（手机）产业园为引领的非苹果手机产业集群，"N"则是河南首家半导体级硅晶圆片生产企业郑州合晶、首个液晶显示面板生产制造项目华锐光电、北斗导航行业龙头合众思壮等一批重点推进项目。

华锐光电液晶显示器件项目历时6个月主厂房封顶，生产线核心设备陆续搬入，2020年底点亮；郑州合晶硅单晶抛光片项目历时15

the whole production line. With the help of the Administrative Committee of the Zhengzhou Airport Economy Zone, the Commerce Bureau and the Park Operation Center, Zhengzhou Lianchuang Electronics Co., Ltd. has made rapid progress. In one year, the number of employees has grown from 100 to 2,200, achieving a monthly production capacity of 3.5 million mobile phones, the monthly shipment of 10 million image modules, and average monthly sales of 150 million *yuan*. Its products are sold to Samsung, Xiaomi, OPPO, vivo, Transsion, Tesla and other end manufacturers.

Since Foxconn's smart phone project landed in 2010, the Zhengzhou Airport Economy Zone has seized the opportunity of industrial shift and found a way of transformation and development of the electronic information industry with intelligent terminals as a breakthrough. Now more than 100 smart terminal enterprises such as Foxconn, Zhengzhou Lianchuang Electronics Co., Ltd. and Zhengzhou Baojufeng Industrial Co., Ltd. have settled in the Zone, achieving a rapid breakthrough of "from an apple to an orchard". In 2019, the import and export volume of intelligent terminals and their supporting enterprises in the Zhengzhou Airport Economy Zone reached 346.406 billion *yuan*, accounting for 96.56% of the total import and export volume of the whole region. From 2011 to 2019, the cumulative mobile phone shipments in the whole region exceeded 1.5 billion, making Henan the largest mobile phone producer in China after Guangdong.

"Success will come when conditions are ripe." Wang Fei, director of the Commerce Bureau of the Zhengzhou Airport Economy Zone, commented on the immediate changes. "The intelligent terminal industry in the Zhengzhou Airport Economy Zone is gradually expanding from whole machine assembly operated by light assets to deep processing fields such as new display and camera modules invested by heavy assets, and is extending to the chip, panel, R & D and high-end manufacturing in the upstream of the industrial chain, and is also spreading to the application industrial chain such as Intelligent Network Connect, smart home and smart medical."

Every round of technological change breeds great development opportunities. If we can grasp and use them well, we can achieve a leap forward or even catching-up development of the industry. In the 1970s and 1980s, Japan greatly

个月全面投产,彻底改变了航空港实验区"缺芯少屏"的局面,2020年订单量增长500%;通过资本运作,引进上市公司合众思壮在航空港实验区创建北斗产业园、北斗研究院,开启北斗定位导航产业发展序幕。除此之外,先进微电子半导体封装划片机、东微电子先进集成电路芯片靶材、浪潮郑州生产基地、博众精工智能装备及自动化生产、中国电信中部智慧基地、771研究所第三代半导体生产制造基地等项

航空港实验区电子信息先进制造业集群(左上:郑州合晶 右上:华锐光电 左下:北斗产业园 右下:博众精工)

Advanced Electronic Information Manufacturing Clusters in the Zhengzhou Airport Economy Zone〔Upper Left: Wafer Works (Zhengzhou) Corp. Upper Right: Huarui Optoelectronic Lower Left: Beidou Industrial Park Lower Right: Bozhong Seiko〕

narrowed its gap with the United States in the electronic information industry by developing large-scale integrated circuits. At the beginning of the 21st century, South Korea and Taiwan seized the opportunity of the "display revolution" and rose rapidly in the field of display devices by vigorously developing TFT- LCD technology. Nowadays, a new round of scientific and technological revolution is booming in the world, which brings an opportunity to "overtake on the bend" for the adjustment of economic structure and the transition to new from old economic engines in developing countries.

How can the advantages of labor and capital, technology and the markets be put together to continuously integrate various resources across industries, regions and borders, so as to inject "glue" into the industrial chain and supply chain and boost the manufacturing industry to a higher level? This is a question that the Zhengzhou Airport Economy Zone must answer to participate in global industrial chain and supply chain competition and cooperation under the new situation.

In 2018, the Zhengzhou Airport Economy Zone further proposed to pay close attention to the cultivation of world-class advanced electronic information manufacturing clusters represented by intelligent terminals, and established the development concept of "1+1+N". The first "1" is Foxconn's industrial cluster. The second "1" is a non-Apple mobile phone industrial cluster led by the Intelligent Terminal (mobile phone) Industrial Park. The "N" is a number of key promotion projects such as Wafer Works (Zhengzhou) Corp., Henan's first semiconductor-grade silicon wafer manufacturer; Huarui Optoelectronics, the first LCD panel manufacturing project; and Beidou navigation industry leader UniStrong.

The main factory building of the Huarui Optoelectronic LCD Device Project was capped within 6 months. The core pieces of equipment of the production line were moved in one after another and were put into use at the end of 2020. It took 15 months for the Wafer Works (Zhengzhou) Corp., Silicon Single Crystal Smash Project to be put into full production, which completely changed the situation of "lack of core and less screen" in the Zhengzhou Airport Economy Zone, and the order volume increased by 500% in 2020. Through a capital operation, a listed company called UniStrong was introduced to establish the Beidou Industrial Park, the Beidou Research Institute in the Zhengzhou Airport

目相继签约落地。

为抢占新一轮产业竞争制高点,实现智能终端等优势产业"二次生长",航空港实验区把电子信息产业作为参与全球产业链供应链分工的战略之举,制定《以智能终端为代表的电子信息产业三年行动计划(2020—2022年)》,坚持龙头企业发展与产业集群培育并重,实施"千百亿级产业集群"培育行动,通过完善平台功能、创新招商模式、做优双创生态、强化企业服务,力争到2022年,达产60家以上整机制造企业、70家以上关键零部件企业、10家以上研发设计类企业,全区电子信息产业产值突破4000亿元,构建富士康强大"雁阵"、智能终端出口基地、新型显示、半导体、北斗导航、物联网等特色鲜明的电子信息产业园区。

北斗产业园生产线
The Assembly Line in Beidou Industrial Park

蓝图已经擘画,路线图已经绘就。相信在不远的未来,航空港实验区将在智能终端、光电显示、集成电路、智能装配、智慧物联等电子信息全产业生态链领域实现更大突破。

Economy Zone, which marked the buildup to the development of the Beidou positioning and navigation industry. In addition, the advanced microelectronics semiconductor packaging scribing machine, East Microelectronics' advanced integrated circuit chip, the Inspur Zhengzhou production base, Bozhong Seiko's intelligent equipment and automatic production, China Telecom central smart base, the third generation semiconductor manufacturing base of the 771 Research Institute and other projects have been signed one after another.

To seize the commanding heights of the new round of industrial competition and to realize the "secondary growth" of advantageous industries such as intelligent terminals, the Zhengzhou Airport Economy Zone regards the electronic information industry as a strategy to participate in the division of labor in the global industrial chain and supply chain. It has formulated *The Three-Year Action Plan for the Electronic Information Industry Represented by Intelligent Terminals (2020-2022)*. By attaching equal importance to the development of leading enterprises and to the cultivation of industrial clusters, the Zhengzhou Airport Economy Zone has implemented the "Tens of Billions of Industrial Clusters" program. By improving the functions of the platform, innovating investment promotion, creating an excellent and innovative environment, and strengthening business services, the zone strives to produce more than 60 machine manufacturing enterprises, more than 70 key parts enterprises and more than 10 R & D design enterprises by 2022. The output value of the electronic information industry in the whole region will exceed 400 billion *yuan*. The Zhengzhou Airport Economy Zone will build Foxconn's powerful "Wild Goose Queue", and an intelligent terminal export base, along with new display, semiconductor, Beidou navigation, Internet of Things and other distinctive electronic information industrial parks.

Both the blueprint and the roadmap have been drawn. The Zhengzhou Airport Economy Zone will achieve greater breakthroughs in the ecological chain of the electronic information industry such as intelligent terminals, photoelectric displays, integrated circuits, intelligent assembly, and intelligent Internet of Things in the near future.

三、产业腾飞画蓝图

2019年4月9日,郑州国际会展中心轩辕厅,由河南省人民政府、中华人民共和国商务部、中国国际贸易促进委员会、中国人民对外友好协会联合主办,以"开放合作、中原出彩"为主题的第十三届中国河南国际投资贸易洽谈会隆重开幕。作为本届投洽会的专题活动,第一届郑州国际生物药发展高峰论坛同期举行。

第一届郑州国际生物药发展高峰论坛开幕
The First Zhengzhou International Biopharmaceutical Development Summit

这是河南第一次举办如此高规格的生物医药领域专业论坛。全国政协副主席、农工党中央常务副主席何维,河南省副省长何金平,全国政协常委、河南省政协副主席、农工党省委主委高体健,以及郑州市、航空港实验区主要领导出席会议,与300余家知名创新药企、资本方及高校科研人员现场交流。

人群中,个子不高、看起来有些瘦小的钟南并不引人注意,但他却是此次论坛的主要发起人之一。这位北京大学结构生物学博士,曾在加

III. A Blueprint for Industrial Take-off

On April 9, 2019, the 13th China Henan International Investment and Trade Fair with the theme of "Open Cooperation for a Brilliant Central Plains" was grandly opened in the Xuanyuan Hall of the Zhengzhou International Convention and Exhibition Center. The event was jointly sponsored by the Henan Provincial People's Government, the Ministry of Commerce of the People's Republic of China, the China Council for the Promotion of International Trade and by the Chinese People's Association for Friendship with Foreign Countries. As a special event of this conference, the first Zhengzhou International Biopharmaceutical Development Summit Forum was held simultaneously.

This was the first time Henan had held such a high-level professional forum in the field of biomedicine. He Wei, vice-chair of the National Committee of the Chinese People's Political Consultative Conference and executive vice-chair of the Central Committee of the Agricultural Labor Party; He Jinping, vice-governor of Henan Province; Gao Tijian, member of the Standing Committee of the National Committee of the Chinese People's Political Consultative Conference, vice-chair of the Henan Provincial Committee of the Chinese People's Political Consultative Conference and chairperson of the Provincial Committee of the Agricultural Labor Party; as well as the leaders of the city of Zhengzhou and the Zhengzhou Airport Economy Zone attended the meeting and exchanged views with more than three hundred attendees, including executives of well-known innovative pharmaceutical companies, investors, and university researchers.

In the crowd, Zhong Nan, who is not tall and looks a little thin, was not noticeable, but he is one of the main sponsors of this forum. As a Ph.D. in Structural Biology from Peking University, Professor Zhong has been engaged in high-throughput development and application research from genes to monoclonal antibodies as a postdoctoral researcher at the Structural Genome Alliance (SGC) of the University of Toronto, Canada. He established and presided over a high-throughput monoclonal antibody development platform. After returning to China, he has worked as a senior scientist for well-known pharmaceutical companies and has introduced and developed a number of innovative drugs used

拿大多伦多大学结构基因组联盟（SGC）以博士后研究员身份从事"从基因到单克隆抗体"高通量开发与应用研究，建立并主持高通量单克隆抗体开发平台，回国后曾在知名药企任资深科学家，引进开发多个一类抗肿瘤和呼吸道病毒创新药物。

钟南的另一个身份是郑州临空生物医药园董事长、总经理。2016年，36岁的钟南作为特聘高级人才来到航空港实验区，受命主导郑州临空生物医药园的定位、规划、建设和后续运营。从承揽这项工作起，钟南就深知，使命神圣，责任重大，意义非凡。

于是，他带领团队东奔西走，到国内外顶尖产业园进行调研考察。在反复调研、学习借鉴、充分论证的基础上，钟南得出结论：拼研发能力、拼学术力量、拼资金，郑州比不过北上广深，但郑州有郑州的优势。

郑州临空生物医药园风姿初现

The Life Zhengzhou Park

to treat Class I tumors along with respiratory viruses.

Another of Zhong Nan's titles is the chairperson and general manager of the Life Zhengzhou Park. In 2016, 36-year-old Zhong Nan came to the Zhengzhou Airport Economy Zone as a senior specialist, and he was appointed to lead the positioning, planning, construction and follow-up operations of the Life Zhengzhou Park. Since undertaking this work, Zhong Nan has come to learn that the mission is sacred, the responsibility is great and the significance is greater.

Therefore, he led the team around and went to the top industrial parks both in China and abroad for investigation and research. On the basis of repeated investigation, learning and full demonstration, Zhong Nan came to this conclusion: in terms of research and development capability, academic strength and capital, Zhengzhou is not as good as Beijing, Shanghai, Guangzhou and Shenzhen, but Zhengzhou has the advantages of its own. Located in the hinterland of the Central Plains, Zhengzhou is not only an important node of the Belt and Road Initiative development strategy, but also an important comprehensive transportation hub, trade and logistics center and inland import and export city, with outstanding location advantages. It has the superposition of multiple policies such as being designated a national demonstration base for entrepreneurship and innovation, a cross-border e-commerce comprehensive experimental zone, a free trade zone, a pilot zone for introducing talents and also a national high-tech bio-industry base. Zhengzhou also has market demand and labor advantages brought about by the huge demographic dividend in the Central Plains region, the excellent air transportation conditions in the airport region and a stable industrial foundation. All these factors have provided important support for the development of the biomedical industry.

After some comparative debate, the development path of "production-oriented R&D" gradually became clear—taking the scarce industrialized public service platform in the market as the breakthrough point to build a public service system for medicine, medical treatment and medical science. Through the advantages of policies and platforms, enterprises that have completed basic research in the field of biomedicine, developed to the stage of industrialization and have core technology products will be attracted to establish production-oriented research and development bases in the zone.

地处中原腹地，不仅是"一带一路"发展战略的重要节点，也是重要的综合交通枢纽、商贸物流中心和内陆进出口大市，区位优势突出；国家级"双创"示范基地、跨境电商综试区、自由贸易区、引智试验区等多重政策叠加，更是国家高技术生物产业基地；还有中原地区巨大的人口红利带来的市场需求和劳动力优势，空港地区绝佳的航空运输条件和逐渐稳固的产业基础……这些都为生物医药产业的发展提供了重要支撑。

一番比较论证之后，主打"生产型研发"的发展道路逐渐清晰——以市场稀缺的产业化公共服务平台为切入点，构建医药、医疗、医学三医公共服务体系，通过政策和平台优势，吸引在生物医药领域已完成基础研究、进入产业化阶段且具有核心技术产品的企业来区建立生产型研发基地。

在钟南博士主导下，2017年5月，郑州临空生物医药园开工建设，从无到有构建生物医药产业环境：

专业生产厂房层高3.8米至7.2米不等、承重$10kN/m^2$，全部配备双回路电蒸汽站、废水处理站、专属物流体系等专业配套，同步建设展示中心、孵化中心、中试组团、专家公寓、企业总部等生活配套；

搭建全流程公共技术服务平台，支持企业获得环评、GLP、GMP等资质认证，解决企业产业化核心瓶颈，力争硬件设施和运营水平双双达到国际标准；

依托50亿元母基金，与一线基金合作，构建覆盖Angel、VC、PE、Pre-IPO的完整市场化投资体系，投资入股，降低企业重资产投入负担……

生物医药行业是典型的"三高"行业——高技术、高投入、高风险。通常，一种药物从开发到上市需要耗时超过12年，耗费15亿美元。"新药研究开发耗资大、耗时长、难度大，很多有想法、有能力的科研团队迫于资金、市场压力难以为继，我们的目标就是打造一个共生共享的园区，企业只要有idea，就能在这里将梦想实现。"钟南说。

Under the leadership of Dr. Zhong Nan, Life Zhengzhou Park started construction to build a biomedical industry environment from scratch in May 2017.

The professional production plant has a floor height of between 3.8 meters and 7.2 meters and a load bearing capacity of $10KN/m^2$. It is equipped with professional supporting facilities such as a double-circuit electric steam plant, a wastewater treatment plant and an exclusive logistics system. It is also equipped with living facilities such as an exhibition center, an incubation center, a pilot scale production group, apartments for experts and enterprise headquarters.

A full-process public technical service platform is to be built in order to support enterprises in obtaining qualification certifications, such as EIA, GLP, and GMP; solve the core bottleneck of the industrialization of enterprises; and strive to meet international standards in hardware facilities and operational level.

Relying on five billion *yuan* in start-up capital and cooperating with first-line funds, a complete market-oriented investment system covering Angel, VC, PE and Pre-IPO will be built and shares will be purchased to reduce the burden of heavy asset investment of enterprises.

The biomedical industry is a typical "three highs" industry—high technology, high investment and high risk. Usually, it takes more than 12 years for a drug to be developed and put on the market, costing 1.5 billion US dollars. "The research and development of new drugs is costly, time-consuming and difficult. Many thoughtful and capable research teams are unsustainable due to the market and capital pressure. Our goal is to build a symbiotic and shared park, where enterprises can realize their dreams as long as they have an idea." Zhong Nan said.

Aiming at the commanding heights of the industry, the park layout seeks to spur innovation in the four core industries of drug research, development and production, cell technology and application, IVD third-party testing, and high-end medical devices. By recruiting the strong and attracting the excellent, a trend is taking shape—more leading enterprises with high-quality products are gathering here. In 2020 alone, the Life Zhengzhou Park had added 173 high-quality projects, 37 contract projects, and 23 leading pharmaceutical enterprises such as Gmax Biopharm International Limited, Leadingpharm Medical Techonology, Meitaibao Biopharmaceutical Co., Ltd., Gensciences and Tetranov

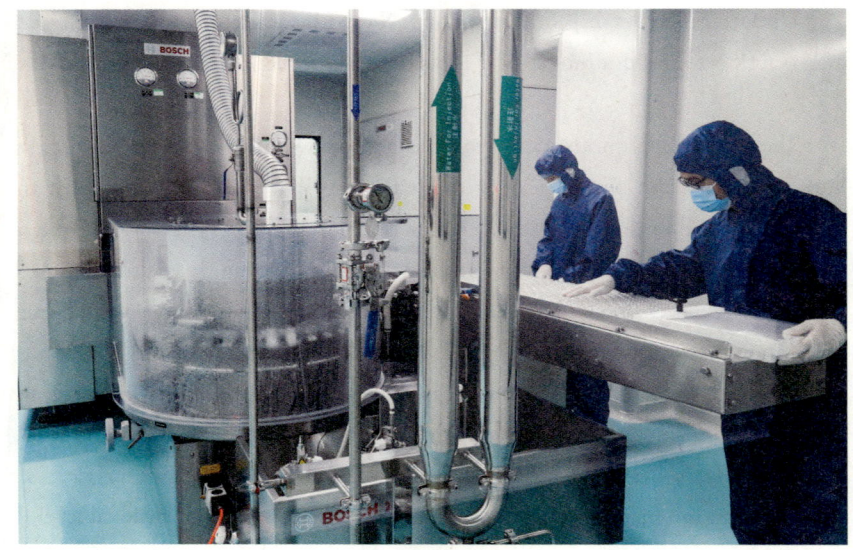

研究人员正在进行试验
Researchers are conducting experiments.

  瞄准产业制高点，园区布局创新药物研发生产、细胞技术及应用、IVD/第三方检测和高端医疗器械四大核心产业，招强引优，初步形成龙头牵引、高质集聚之势。2020 年，郑州临空生物医药园已累计储备优质项目 173 个，签约项目 37 家，通过专家评审会排队入园项目 53 个，鸿运华宁、新领先、美泰宝、晟斯生物、泰基鸿诺等 23 家医药龙头企业落地并陆续投产。一批针对重大、急恶性疾病（如肺动脉高压、糖尿病、血友病、肿瘤、肝炎等）的一类创新药陆续进入临床研究，将在未来两三年内全球上市，成为中国医药创新的一面旗帜。

  步入郑州临空生物医药园大门，一座打破传统中国建筑对称格局、呈内外双螺旋上升造型的建筑首先映入眼帘。这里是郑州临空生物医药园展示中心。其设计灵感来自 DNA 结构，寓意生物医药行业与生俱来的基因和特征：创新、前沿、生长、永无止境……

Biopharm Limited. In addition, another 53 projects were lined up to enter the park pending expert review meetings. A number of innovative drugs for major and acute diseases such as pulmonary hypertension, diabetes, hemophilia, cancer, and hepatitis have started clinical research one after another and will enter global market in the next two to three years, becoming a beacon of Chinese medical innovation.

Entering the doors of the Life Zhengzhou Park, a building that breaks the symmetrical pattern of traditional Chinese architecture, the rising shape of a double helix first comes into view. This is the exhibition center of the Life Zhengzhou Park. Its design was inspired by the structure of DNA, signifying genes and the characteristics of the biomedical industry: innovative, groundbreaking, growing, and endless.

During the year when the exhibition center opened to welcome guests, leaders at all levels in Henan Province and the city of Zhengzhou, as well as leaders from pharmaceutical companies and investors from all over the world visited and inspected the park hundreds of times.

On December 28, 2018, at the signing ceremony for the first batch of enterprises entering the park, Dr. Jing Shuqian, a native of Henan's Pingdingshan who worked for world-renowned biopharmaceutical companies BMS and Amgen for many years, signed an incubation services agreement with Life Zhengzhou Park on behalf of Zhengzhou Gmax Biopharm International Limited Biomedical Engineering Co., Ltd..

Gmax Biopharm International Limited was founded in 2010. Headquartered in Hangzhou, China, it is an innovative biomedical company that was jointly established by senior returnees and domestic entrepreneurs. It is also one of the few pharmaceutical companies in the world that create new original antibody drugs in the field of GPCR (G protein coupled receptor). The company is mainly committed to the research, development and industrialization of new antibody drugs for cardiovascular problems, metabolic system problems and cancer. In 2017, Gmax Biopharm International Limited set up a branch in the Zhengzhou Airport Economy Zone. The newly established Zhengzhou branch focuses on the late-stage development and industrialization of products, which is different from Hangzhou Headquarters' focus on the screening and early evaluation of candidate

郑州临空生物医药园一期鸟瞰图
An Aerial View of the First Phase of the Life Zhengzhou Park

从展示中心开门迎客的一年间,这里先后迎来河南省、郑州市各级领导,以及来自世界各地的医药企业、资本方上百次参观考察。

2018年12月28日,首批入园企业签约仪式现场,祖籍河南平顶山、曾在全球知名生物制药企业BMS和Amgen工作多年的景书谦博士,代表郑州鸿运华宁生物医药工程有限公司与郑州临空生物医药园签署孵化服务协议。

鸿运华宁成立于2010年,总部位于中国杭州,是一家由资深海归和国内企业家共同发起成立的创新性生物医药企业,也是世界上GPCR(G蛋白偶联受体)领域屈指可数的原创抗体新药企业之一,主要致力于心血管、代谢系统以及癌症的抗体新药研发与产业化。2017年,鸿运华宁在航空港实验区筹建分公司。新成立的郑州公司,侧重产品的后期开发和产业化,与杭州总部侧重候选药物的筛选和前期评价相区分,目的是利用不同地区的优势优化资源配置,实现降本增效。

drugs. The purpose of the new branch is to optimize the allocation of resources by utilizing the advantages of different regions and to realize cost savings and increases in efficiency.

"The late-stage development and industrialization of products depend on the amplification of pharmaceutical technology and the matching of production and manufacturing conditions, which usually require heavy investment in assets. The Life Zhengzhou Park has provided very strong support in these areas." As the first batch of innovative drug experts who returned to China to start businesses, Jing Shuqian introduced Gmax Biopharm International Limited to friends around him more than once.

In December 2020, the project of Biological Innovative Drug Production Base was started in the Zhengzhou Airport Economy Zone. The Base adopts the policy of "Hangzhou as the Innovation and Policy Source, Zhengzhou the Industrial Transformation", and the two sites develop together. After completion, it will become the first large-scale production base of antibody drugs in the Central Plains that meets the international cGMP standard, and will achieve the industrialization of many internationally leading and groundbreaking innovative antibody drugs for Gmax Biopharm International Limited. The expected annual output value of full production may reach ninety billion *yuan*, and the annual tax contribution may exceed nine billion *yuan*. This is the first national large-scale production base project of Class I innovative drugs undertaken by the Zhengzhou Airport Economy Zone, and it is also an important step in promoting the high-level opening up and high-quality development of the region.

At present, Gmax Biopharm International Limited has successfully prepared and screened eleven new antibody drugs for severe diseases such as Diabetes mellitus Type II, obesity, pulmonary hypertension and cancer, using the world-leading exclusive pharmaceutical GPCR (G protein coupled receptor) antibody preparation and screening technology platform. Among them, GMA301, the world's first new antibody drug for treating pulmonary hypertension, was fully launched on July 15, 2020. "We plan to build a global product manufacturing and supply center in the Zhengzhou Airport Economy Zone, and gain NASDAQ listing in the next two to three years!" Jing Shuqian is full of confidence when talking about the future development plan.

"产品后期开发和产业化依赖于药品工艺放大和生产制造条件配套,通常都需要重资产的投入,郑州临空生物医药园在这些方面提供了非常强劲的支持。"作为最早一批回国创业的创新药专家,景书谦不止一次向身边的朋友推介。

2020年12月,鸿运华宁郑州生物创新药生产基地项目在航空港实验区启动。基地采用"杭州创新策源,郑州产业转化"模式,两地协同发展。建成后,将成为中原首个符合国际cGMP标准的抗体药物大规模生产基地,实现鸿运华宁多个国际领先、具有突破性疗效抗体创新药的产业化。满产预期年产值达900亿元,年税收贡献超90亿元。这是航空港实验区启动的第一个国家一类创新药大规模生产基地项目,也是推动区域高水平开放和高质量发展的重要一步。

目前,利用具备国际领先水平的独家药用GPCR(G蛋白偶联受体)抗体制备和筛选技术平台,鸿运华宁已成功制备和筛选出11个针对Ⅱ型糖尿病、肥胖、肺动脉高压、恶性肿瘤等重症疾病的抗体新药。其中,全球首个治疗肺动脉高压的抗体新药GMA301中美国际多中心临床试验已于2020年7月15日全面启动。"我们计划在航空港实验区打造面向全球的产品制造供应中心,未来两到三年实现美国纳斯达克上市!"谈及未来的发展规划,景书谦信心满满。

园区在孵企业郑州美港高科生物科技有限公司,为罕见病、重症病患者带来了福音。脑卒中,又称中风,是由于脑部血管病变导致血管闭塞或破裂,从而造成患者功能上缺损的一种疾病,致死、致残率高。大多数患者临床使用的金属不可降解支架,植入后成为一个脑血管内的异物存留一生,且需要终生用药维持,不但极为痛苦,手术及后续治疗费用昂贵,给患者及家庭带来沉重的精神和经济负担。

美港高科自主研发的完全可降解脑血管支架,植入患者脑血管一年后即可完全降解,无须取出或再次手术就能使患者恢复正常的生活状态。该项目依托郑州大学和国内顶尖研发团队,将以超越欧美一代的领先技

Zhengzhou Meigang High Tech Biotechnology Co., Ltd., an incubated enterprise in the park, has brought good news to patients with rare diseases and severe diseases. Cerebral apoplexy, also known as a stroke, is a disease caused by blockage in a vein or by a rupture caused by cerebral vascular diseases, resulting in functional defects in patients, often leading to disability and death. The metal non-degradable stent used by most patients is a foreign body that remains in the cerebral vessels for the rest of the patient's life, which requires lifelong medication maintenance. It is not only extremely painful, but also expensive for surgery and follow-up treatment, bringing heavy mental and economic burdens to patients and their families.

However, the completely degradable cerebrovascular stent developed by Zhengzhou Meigang High Tech Biotechnology Co., Ltd. disappears after being in the patient's cerebrovascular system for one year, and the patient can return to normal living conditions without removal or reoperation. Relying on Zhengzhou University and the top domestic research and development teams, the project will surpass the leading technology of the European and American models to enable patients in China and even in the world to use the most advanced and inexpensive degradable cerebrovascular stents made in China.

How far are driverless vehicles from us? On a winter day in 2019, more than 400 automobile enthusiasts gathered in the Zhengzhou Airport Economy Zone to feel the charm of driverless technology at the 2019 China (Zhengzhou) Automobile Intelligent Technology Conference.

With the theme of "5G Vehicle Alliance Leading the Future with Wisdom", the conference aimed to build a forum integrating industry forums, authoritative competitions, and promotion and application demonstration, so as to make the city prosperous by competitions, promote production by meetings, benefit the people by exhibitions, and help Zhengzhou new energy vehicles and the intelligent networked automobile industry to develop with high quality. Participating organizations included government departments, such as the Chinese Academy of Engineering, the National Intelligent Networked Automobile Innovation Center, and the Automobile Smart Travel Research Association; universities and other scientific research institutes; traditional vehicle companies such as China Automotive (Beijing), Changan Automobile and Yutong Bus; and information

术,让中国乃至世界的患者用上国产最先进且价格低廉的可降解脑血管支架。

无人驾驶离我们有多远？2019年的一个冬日,400余名汽车发烧友聚集在航空港实验区,在2019中国（郑州）汽车智能科技大会上感受无人驾驶的科技魅力。

大会以"5G车联·智领未来"为主题,旨在打造集行业论坛、权威赛事、推广应用示范于一体的行业平台,以赛兴城、以会促产、以展惠民,助力郑州新能源汽车及智能网联汽车产业高质量发展。参会单位既有政府单位,如中国工程院、国家智能网联汽车创新中心、汽车智慧出行研究会等高校和科研所,也有国汽（北京）、长安汽车、宇通客车等主流整车企业,以及华为、中移物联网、北京合众思壮等信息科技与互联网公司。

作为智能汽车科技的年度盛事,展会云集了国内国际市场最前端的科技创新成果。室内展览部分,中国移动和中国电信5G+各场景应用,中国联通企业上云,中国铁塔标准化产品＋一揽子解决方案,中兴通讯综合通信解决方案,郑州航空港兴港智慧城市有限公司智慧城市项目等,包括车身电子、自动驾驶、智能网联技术、新能源汽车技术、测试技术、汽车材料等智能汽车前沿科技成果一一展示。而在园博园室外动态展览示范区,寒冷的天气依然无法阻挡市民对智能车辆的新奇与体验。预约体验区一早就排起了长长的队伍,参观的市民都想在第一时间零距离接触只有在科幻大片中才能看到的无人驾驶车辆。

郑州宇通客车股份有限公司参加展示的是无人驾驶公交车,可容纳8—12名乘客的公交车,不但可以精确进站、换道避障,发现对面来车还能自主会车。结合云控系统,公交车最高时速可达40km/h,可为园区、景区等限定区域提供约车、班车等不同模式的自动驾驶接驳服务。

北京合众思壮科技股份有限公司展示了安装自动驾驶系统的农机,农机从起步加速到自动调头、农机具的提升下降、自动转弯,再到结束

technology and Internet companies, such as Huawei, China Mobile Internet of Things and UniStrong (Beijing).

As an annual event of intelligent vehicles technology, the exhibition gathered the most advanced scientific and technological innovations in the domestic and international markets. In the indoor exhibition section, there were China Mobile and China Telecom 5G + application on different scenes, China Unicom enterprises on the cloud, China Tower Standardized Products + Package Solutions, ZTE Corporation (Zhongxing Telecommunication Equipment) Integrated Communication Solutions, the Smart City Project of Zhengzhou Airport Xinggang Smart City Co., Ltd., among many others. Wearable electronics, automated driving, intelligent networking technology, new energy vehicle technology, measuring and testing techniques, automotive materials and other cutting-edge scientific and technological achievements of smart cars were all on display. At the outdoor dynamic exhibition demonstration area of the Garden Expo Park, the cold weather couldn't stop the residents from experiencing the novelty of intelligent vehicles. There was a long queue in the reservation area early in the morning, and the visitors wanted to get an up-close look at driverless vehicles that could usually only be seen in sci-fi blockbusters.

Zhengzhou Yutong Bus Co., Ltd. participated in the exhibition of driverless buses, which can accommodate eight to twelve passengers. The buses can not only accurately enter the stop, change lanes and avoid obstacles, but automatically maneuver around vehicles coming towards them from the opposite direction. Combined with the cloud control system, the buses can reach speeds of forty kilometers per hour. Therefore, the buses can provide different modes of automatic driving service such as car hailing and shuttle bus for limited areas such as parks and scenic spots.

Beijing UniStrong Technology Co., Ltd. demonstrated agricultural machinery equipped with an automatic driving system. The truly driverless process, which includes starting and acceleration, lifting and lowering of agricultural implements, automatic turning, and automatic parking, was coherent and smooth.

Beijing Xiangzhi Technology Co., Ltd. is an intelligent driving system manufacturer, and its intelligent driving "brain" is used in many industries. Automated car ferries, robotic sweepers, intelligent buses, and intelligent patrol

2019中国（郑州）汽车智能科技大会上展出的无人驾驶车辆和新能源汽车
Driverless vehicles and new energy vehicles on display at the China (Zhengzhou) Automobile Intelligent Technology Conference in 2019.

时的自动停车，整个流程连贯顺畅，真正实现了全程无人作业。

享智科技是一家智能驾驶系统供应商，其智能驾驶"大脑"更是应用于多个行业，无人驾驶摆渡车、无人清扫车、智能巴士、智能巡逻车等，都让市民连连称赞科技的进步。

近年来，人工智能、5G、物联网等一系列技术创新，正引领和驱动着整个汽车行业的发展。汽车正在从传统交通工具加速向移动智能终端，多功能的移动空间演进。前瞻技术与汽车的高度融合，衍生出自动驾驶、

cars have all made people praise the progress of science and technology.

In recent years, a series of technological innovations such as artificial intelligence, 5G and Internet of Things are driving the development of the entire automobile industry. Automobiles are evolving from traditional vehicles to mobile intelligent terminals and multifunctional mobile spaces. The high integration of forward-looking technologies and automobiles has spawned a variety of new business models such as automatic driving and shared travel. The development of intelligent networked automobiles shows the positive trends of accelerating breakthroughs in core technologies, accelerating improvement of basic support and maturing industrial environment, and shows that a new automobile era is imminent.

The trinity of "meeting, competition and exhibition" of the 2019 China (Zhengzhou) Automobile Intelligent Technology Conference came just in time, and the "Zhengzhou Voice" of building an intelligent networked automobile ecosystem was officially issued. Driven by leading enterprises and the continuous gathering of upstream and downstream industrial chains, the Zhengzhou Airport Economy Zone will build an important national intelligent network and new energy automobile industry base.

At the meeting, the Administrative Committee of the Zhengzhou Airport Economy Zone signed strategic cooperation framework agreements with five telecom companies such as China Mobile, China Unicom and China Telecom, and a number of intelligent networked enterprises such as Tianmai Technology and UniStrong, worth a total of 4.5 billion *yuan*. According to the agreements, in the future, the two sides will carry out extensive cooperation in 5G construction, new smart city construction, new energy, Internet of Things, intelligent manufacturing and other fields to jointly promote the development of the big data industry in the Zhengzhou Airport Economy Zone and the construction of a smart city. This also indicates that the intelligent networked automobile industry chain in the Zhengzhou Airport Economy Zone is becoming more and more complete, the development space is expanding, and the agglomeration effect is becoming more and more prominent.

If the industrial implementation in the early stage mainly depends on undertaking coastal industrial transfer and accumulating the driving force of

共享出行等多种新的商业模式，全球智能网联汽车发展呈现出核心技术加速突破、基础支撑加快完善、产业生态渐趋成熟的良好态势，一个新的汽车时代呼之欲出。

2019中国（郑州）汽车智能科技大会"会、赛、展"三位一体，恰逢其时，正式发出了构建智能网联汽车生态圈的"郑州声音"。通过龙头企业带动和上下游产业链的不断集聚，航空港实验区将打造全国重要的智能网联和新能源汽车产业基地。

会上，航空港实验区管委会分别与中国移动、中国联通、中国电信等5家通讯运营商和天迈科技、合众思壮等多家智能网联企业签订了战略合作框架协议，签约总金额达45亿元。根据协议，未来双方将在5G建设、新型智慧城市建设、新能源、物联网、智能制造等多个领域开展广泛合作，共同促进航空港实验区大数据产业发展，推进智慧城市建设。这也标志着航空港实验区智能网联汽车产业链日趋完整，发展空间不断扩展，聚集效应愈加凸显。

如果说航空港实验区前期的产业导入主要依靠的是承接沿海产业转移，积聚了城市发展的原动力，那么在国际国内环境风云变幻、全球市场分工加速调整的背景下，不沿边、不靠海的航空港实验区正趁着航空经济的东风，瞄准生物医药、新能源、商贸会展等系列朝阳产业，走出一条科技、绿色、健康的现代临空经济发展道路。

如今的航空港实验区犹如一个大舞台，吸引各类新兴产业八方登场。先进制造业、现代服务业融合发展，航空物流、跨境电商、新能源汽车、生物医药、北斗导航、智能装备、新型显示、新基建八大产业集群各显神通……以航空港实验区为"龙头""引领"，河南开放的大门越开越大、开放的步伐越走越快、开放的环境越来越好，中原大地已经成为投资兴业的热土，实现梦想的乐园。

urban development, the Zhengzhou Airport Economy Zone, which is not along the border or by the sea, is taking advantage of the aviation economy, aiming at a series of emerging industries such as biomedicine, new energy, trade and exhibition, and embarking on a scientific, green and healthy modern airport economic development path in the context of a changing international and domestic environment and accelerating adjustment to the division of international market.

Today's Zhengzhou Airport Economy Zone is like a big stage, attracting all kinds of emerging industries from all directions. With the integration and development of advanced manufacturing and modern service industries, eight industrial clusters, namely aviation logistics, cross-border e-commerce, new energy vehicles, biomedicine, Beidou navigation, intelligent equipment, new display and new infrastructure, show their magical powers. With the Zhengzhou Airport Economy Zone as the "leader", Henan's doors are opening wider and wider to the world, the pace of opening is getting faster and faster, and the open environment is getting better and better. The Central Plains has become a hot spot for investment and development and a paradise for realizing dreams.

第三章

航空大都市

Chapter 3

Aviation Metropolis

"郑州航空港区是一个因一开始就具备出色的顶层规划而取得成功的案例,将来会成为全国乃至全球范围内建设航空都市的典范。""全球航空经济第一人"、航空都市理论模型创立者、航空港实验区首席顾问、航都院院长约翰·卡萨达盛赞航空港实验区出生即出色。"我要让'ZAEZ'(航空港实验区)的名字叫响全世界,并愿意为郑州航空港做全球代言人。"

经年奋飞路,今日大都市。自 2013 年获批至今,航空港实验区寻着陆上丝绸之路的足迹,打开了各国友好交往的窗口。枢纽建设提档升级,开放平台持续完善,综合实力快速攀升。这个满载希望、众所瞩目的"春天的故事"已经唱响,一幅承载着"交通大枢纽、开放大门户、航空大都市"的国际化生态宜居宜业航空新城画卷,正在此徐徐展开。

一、"飞"出一座大都市

经济全球化浪潮袭来,时间,成为竞争的重要因素。航空运输更加适应国际贸易距离长、空间范围广、时效要求高等需求,让信息和金融的流通、交换进入零时距,成为继海运、河运、铁路和公路运输之后驱动经济发展的"第五冲击波"。正如《航空大都市:我们未来的生活方式》中所说:"长期以来,城市的轮廓和命运都取决于交通运输方式。如今,是航空运输的时代。""空中丝绸之路"又赋予郑州更大的机遇,航空港实验区,无疑站在了风口中的风口。

在约翰·卡萨达看来,如果将航空都市比作一个同心圆,机场则位于同心圆的圆心,随着机场辐射范围的扩大,同心圆辐射的范围也随之扩大。在如今的航空港实验区或可一窥全貌。

在这里,进出口岸、产业园区和保税仓库绕机场密布,跨境商品贸易交易繁忙;在这里,你可以见到来自世界各地,各种肤色、讲各种语言的人们,也可以方便搭乘飞机、高铁、地铁、汽车等任何交通方式去

"The Zhengzhou Airport Economy Zone is a successful case because of its excellent top-level planning from the beginning, and I think it will become a model for the whole country and even the world in the future." John Kasarda, the "first pioneer in the global aviation economy", founder of the theoretical model of the aviation city, principal adviser of the Zhengzhou Airport Economy Zone and president of the Aerotropolis Institute in Zhengzhou, praised the impressiveness of the Zhengzhou Airport Economy Zone. "I want to make the name 'ZAEZ' (Zhengzhou Airport Economy Zone) known all over the world, and I'm willing to be its global spokesperson."

Years of hard work has made today's metropolis. Since its approval in 2013, the Zhengzhou Airport Economy Zone has opened a window for friendly exchanges between countries along the Silk Road. The transportation hub has been upgraded, relevant functions have been continuously improved, and the comprehensive strength of the Zhengzhou Airport Economy Zone has risen rapidly. A song of development, which is full of hope and allure, has been sung, and a scroll painted with the masterpiece of an international and habitable New Aviation City incorporating a major transportation hub, an open channel for collaboration and an aviation metropolis is slowly unfolding here.

I . A Metropolis Rising on Plane Wings

Due to economic globalization, time has become a crucial factor in competition. Compared to traditional modes of transport, air transport is more suitable to meet the needs of just-in-time delivery for international trade, and it boosts the instant circulation and exchange of information and finance. Therefore, air transport has become the fifth driving force behind economic development after sea transport, river transport, railway transport and road transport. As noted in the book *Aviation Metropolis: Our Future Lifestyle*, "For a long time, the structure and destiny of a city has depended on the mode of transportation. Today is the era of air transport." The "Aerial Silk Road" has granted Zhengzhou greater opportunities, and the Zhengzhou Airport Economy Zone undoubtedly stands at the center of these opportunities.

In John Kasarda's view, if an aviation metropolis is compared to a concentric

欣欣向荣的航空港实验区
The Prosperous Zhengzhou Airport Economy Zone

往你想去的任何地方；在这里，不论你来自何方，不分身份、国籍、信仰，都能享受国际化、人性化的设施与服务，在尊重与理解，碰撞与交流中实现人生的价值与梦想。

今天的这一切，早在2013年之时，就已埋下伏笔。2013年3月7日，国务院批复《郑州航空港经济综合实验区发展规划（2013—2025年）》，全国首个航空经济先行区正式起航。

多年后的今天，结出了累累硕果。正如约翰·卡萨达所言，航空都市理论模型在航空港实验区一步步变为现实，逐步发展成为颇具代表性

circle, the airport is its central point. With the expansion of the airport, the range of the concentric circle also grows in proportion to the airport. A glimpse of the Zhengzhou Airport Economy Zone shows this:

Here densely packed import and export ports, industrial parks and bonded warehouses surround the airport, and cross-border trade is busily conducted. You can meet people from everywhere, people of all colors and people who speak in many languages. You can easily take any mode of transportation, be it plane, high-speed train, subway, or car, to go wherever you want. No matter where you come from, regardless of your identity, nationality or creed, you can enjoy international facilities and considerate services, feel fully respected and have your values and dreams realized through exchanges and communication.

The foundation for all of this was laid in 2013. On March 7, 2013, *The Development Planning of the Zhengzhou Airport Economy Zone (2013-2025)* was approved by the State Council, marking the starting point of the first national pilot economy zone.

Today, many years later, it has yielded fruitful results. As John Kasarda said, the theoretical model of an aviation metropolis has gradually become a reality in the Zhengzhou Airport Economy Zone and has gradually developed into a typical "China's Aerotropolis".

Building an interconnected global hub. The driving force of the Zhengzhou Airport Economy Zone has far exceeded that of Zhengzhou and Henan, and the nexus between China and the world has been truly realized with the establishment of the airline network spanning the three major economic zones of Europe, America and Asia and covering major economies in the world, a truck transport network covering more than seventy large and medium-sized cities in China, and the star-shaped high-speed rail network in Zhengzhou.

Opening the door to the world. At present, the most advanced port in inland China has been established in the Zhengzhou Airport Economy Zone, making it one of the most important inland ports in China. In 2020, 639,400 tons of cargo and mail passed through Xinzheng International Airport, making it the sixth busiest airport in terms of cargo in China. In addition, passenger volume at the airport was 21,406,700 people, which ranked 11th in the nation. The airport moved up one place in the national rankings in terms of both passenger and

开放门户，连天接地
The Open Portal Bridges Air and Rail Transportation

的"中国的航空大都市"。

打造与世界互联互通的枢纽建设体系。通过横跨欧美亚三大经济区、覆盖全球主要经济体的航线网络、覆盖全国 70 余座大中城市的卡车航班网络、郑州"米"字形高铁网络，航空港实验区的带动影响力已经远远超出了郑州和河南，真正实现了中国与全球的互联互通。

打开对世界开放的门户。目前，航空港实验区已经建立起内陆地区最为完善的开放口岸，成为中国内陆最重要的开放门户之一。2020 年，

freight transportation, and Xinzheng International Airport remained first in both categories in central China for four consecutive years. The Zhengzhou Airport Economy Zone has explored the path of opening up China's vast inland areas to the outside world.

Building "China's Aerotropolis" brand. In October, 2019, the brand "Zhengzhou Airport Economy Zone" was officially released to the world at the Henan Innovation and Development Conference on Recruiting Experts in the Zhengzhou Airport Economy Zone, and made its debut to the world.

Spreading out the world map, you will see Memphis in the United States, Incheon Airport New Town in South Korea, and Amsterdam in the Netherlands.

繁忙的货运
Bustling Freight

新郑国际机场完成货邮吞吐量 63.94 万吨，全国排名提升至第 6 位；完成旅客吞吐量 2140.67 万人次，全国排名提升至第 11 位，客货运全国排名均晋升 1 位，运输规模连续 4 年保持中部"双第一"。航空港实验区为广大内陆地区探索出了一条对外开放的道路。

塑造"中国的航空大都市"品牌。2019 年 10 月，在中国·河南招才引智创新发展大会航空港实验区招才引智专场发布会上，"中国的航空大都市——郑州航空港经济综合实验区"品牌正式全球发布，开始向世界发声。

摊开全球版图，美国的孟菲斯、韩国仁川空港新城、荷兰的阿姆斯特丹，每一个世界级都市圈都有一座航空都市，每一座航空都市都拥有一个"超级"机场。郑州也不例外。在如今的新郑国际机场，人们从世界各地汇聚在此，又从此飞往全球。步履匆匆的商旅精英，青春洋溢的来往旅客，宽敞明亮的候机楼因他们热闹又舒适。

有人这样形容：步入机场大厅，仿佛到了一条琳琅满目的商业街。中式餐饮、西式美食、咖啡果饮、特产便利、服饰箱包、珠宝工艺……这些设施不仅为旅客提供了方便，更是吸引大量空港旅客最有效的载体，也是体现商业价值最直接的平台。在这里，世界知名品牌汇聚，中英双语的贴心服务，"国际范儿"十足。

当夜幕降临，新郑国际机场便进入另一种繁忙。不同于白天的人流密集、车水马龙，货物是夜晚机场的"主角"。来自全球各地的货物在这里被快速进行分拨，然后运往全国各地。同时，中原地区的特色商品、高端制造业和高附加值农副产品也被迅速装进飞往世界各地的货机。

在新郑国际机场外围区域，那里不仅有高档的品质酒店和甲级写字楼，还有大片的物流仓储区域，为与航空业务相关的企业提供了良好的整体环境。此时的新郑国际机场相当于一个具有强大经济辐射能力的城市经济综合体，自带"经济流量"，带着因航而生的航空港实验区"拥抱世界，迎接未来"。

It seems that every world-class metropolitan area has an aviation metropolis, and every aviation metropolis has a "super" airport. Zhengzhou is no exception. At today's Xinzheng International Airport, people gather from all over the world and fly to other places. Bustling business elites and youthful travelers bring energy and vitality to the spacious and bright terminal buildings.

Some people describe it like this: Entering the airport hall is like walking in a dazzling commercial street. Chinese cuisine and Western cuisine, coffee and fruity beverages, specialty and traditional products and locally produced goods, clothing, bags, and jewelry, businesses of all kinds are gathered here, providing convenience for passengers and attracting a large number of customers for business transactions. Here, world-renowned brands are gathered together, and good services can be enjoyed in both Chinese and English.

When night falls, Xinzheng International Airport demonstrates another level of busyness. Different from the crowded and heavy passenger traffic during the day, cargo is the "star" of the airport at night. Goods from all over the world are quickly distributed here and then transported to all parts of the country. At the same time, special commodities, high-end manufacturing products and high value-added agricultural by-products from the Central Plains region are also quickly loaded into cargo planes that fly around the world.

In the peripheral area of Xinzheng International Airport, there are not only high-grade quality hotels and top-level office buildings, but also large warehouses, providing a good overall environment for aviation-related enterprises. At this time, Xinzheng International Airport is equivalent to a radiant urban economic complex with "huge magnetic effect on the economy" that drives the airport-centered economic zone to "embrace the world and welcome the future."

John Kasarda once said, "The Zhengzhou Airport Economy Zone has developed in a timely construction sequence and along a strategic path. It's a model for global aviation cities." After eight years' construction, an international aviation metropolis connected to the whole world has "taken flight" from the small commercial airport which was once surrounded by scattered villages and farmland. In 2020, the GDP of the Zhengzhou Airport Economy Zone exceeded 100 billion *yuan* for the first time, about 4.9 times more than that of 2012. The total volume of foreign trade exceeded 400 billion *yuan*, accounting for over

约翰·卡萨达曾言："航空港实验区发展始终遵循着非常正确的建设时序和战略路径，是全球航空都市的先驱和典范。"历时 8 年，这里从分散、孤立的村庄与自给式农耕所包围的小型商业机场"飞"出了一座"连天接地、通达全球"的国际化航空大都市。2020 年，航空港实验区生产总值首次突破 1000 亿元，约是 2012 年的 4.9 倍；外贸进出口总额突破 4000 亿元，全省外贸占比持续保持 60% 以上；建成区面积突破 100 平方千米，"十三五"时期每年增加约 10 平方千米；航空货运突破 60 万吨，同比增长 22.5%，达 63.94 万吨，货运量累计增速在全国主要机场中居第 1 位；跨境电商单量突破 1 亿单、货值突破 100 亿元，分别为 1.39 亿单、113.9 亿元，连续 5 年实现翻番式增长。在通向高质量发展道路的孜孜追求中，航空港实验区交出了一份缤纷绚丽的精彩答卷。

"枢"联天下，"产"达四方。叠加国家战略各项政策优势，航空港实验区在内陆地区高水平开放、高质量发展中的辐射力、影响力日益提升，正在从一座机场成长为区域经济发展的新引擎，逐渐成为中原腾飞的"翅膀"、撬动发展的"支点"，快速向国际化现代航空大都市迈进。

河南航空经济时代到来了，这座国际化、现代化、人性化航空大都市的蓝图，比任何时候都来得更为清晰和具体。

60% of the total provincial foreign trade volume. The developed area in the zone exceeded 100 square kilometers, having increased about 10 square kilometers every year during the 13th Five-Year Plan period. Air cargo exceeded 600,000 tons, up 22.5% year-on-year to 639,400 tons, and the cumulative growth rate of freight volume ranked first among major airports in China. The volume of cross-border e-commerce orders exceeded 100 million, and the value of goods exceeded 10 billion *yuan*, which were 139 million orders and 11.39 billion *yuan* respectively, representing a doubling of the value and number of orders for five consecutive years. In the nonstop pursuit of high-quality development, the Zhengzhou Airport Economy Zone has produced wonderful examples.

A hub can unite the world and products can reach everywhere. Thanks to national strategy and preferential policies, the influence of the Zhengzhou Airport Economy Zone in the inland area is increasing day by day, and the Xinzheng International Airport is transforming from an airport to a new engine of regional economic development. The Zhengzhou Airport Economy Zone is gradually becoming a "wing" allowing the Central Plains to take off and a "fulcrum" to spur development, and is rapidly developing into an international modern aviation metropolis.

With the arrival of the era of aviation economics in Henan, the blueprint for this modern, international and people-centered aviation metropolis is clearer and more practical than ever.

二、宜居宜业新高地

2018年12月22日，对于畠店、岗李、野王、双楼王等地的村民们来说，注定是一个永远都无法忘却的日子。

深冬的航空港实验区寒风凛冽，但安置房交付仪式现场却热闹非凡，红色气球拱门喜气洋洋，遍布小区的"欢迎回家"道旗和标语让人倍感亲切，主席台后面火红的背板上"幸福入住、欢迎回家"八个字格外醒目。

当天上午，时任郑州市委常委、航空港实验区党工委书记马健向三官庙办事处党工委书记许林山移交了园博幸福花园、园博美丽港湾两个小区的"金钥匙"，村民们也在这一天接过了新家的钥匙，推开了幸福新生活的大门。

"放以前哪里敢想，俺们野王村几代人生活的黄土地，今儿都成了高楼遍地。"家住野王村的王德军是这次回迁居民的一员，他的这句发自内心的感慨，引发了同村几个人的共鸣，"以前的泥路、瓦房，哪还有踪影，村庄摇身一变成了城市，简直像做梦一样"。

跟王德军一样，"过上像城里人一样的生活"是不少村民最大的心愿。这个心愿在2019年得到了实现，在航空港实验区，约有3.5万居民喜圆安居梦。他们和王德军一家一样，将在区位优越、交通便利、配套完善的新型现代化社区，推开城市新生活的大门，热热闹闹在新家过一个团圆年。

机遇前所未有，挑战也前所未有。如何把一个默默无闻的乡村小镇，打造成新型现代化大都市，推动村民们实现从"村民"到"市民"的转变？

答案是：全域城镇化建设。作为我国首个经国务院批复的航空经济先行区，航空港实验区既是新型城镇化建设的探索者，也是示范者。在建设之初，便提出"全域城镇化"战略，坚持以人为本，加快推进棚户区改造，通过打造一个个高品质的现代化社区，营造"宜居、宜业"的城市新空间。

II. A New Destination That Is Habitable and Business-friendly

December 22, 2018 is a day that will never be forgotten by the villagers of Xiaodian, Gangli, Yewang and Shuanglouwang.

The cold wind was blowing hard in the Zhengzhou Airport Economy Zone in the late winter, but the delivery ceremony for the resettlement homes was a warm scene. The jubilant red balloon arch and flags and the "Welcome Home" banners hung all over the community made people feel nice and warm. The four words "Happy Homecoming! Welcome Home!" on the fire-engine-red plaque behind the podium were particularly eye-catching.

That morning, Ma Jian, then member of the Standing Committee of the Zhengzhou Municipal Committee and the secretary of the Party Working Committee of the Zhengzhou Airport Economy Zone, handed over the golden keys to the Yuanbo Happy Garden and Yuanbo Meili Harbor to Xu Linshan, secretary of the Party Working Committee of the Sanguanmiao Office. The villagers also received the keys to their new homes on that day and opened the doors to happy new lives.

"We never imagined that the land where generations of us lived in Yewang Village would become a place full of high-rise buildings today," said Wang Dejun, a resident of Yewang Village who moved into one of the resettlement homes that day. "There are no traces of dirt roads or tiled houses anymore, and the village has been turned into a city. It feels like a dream coming true." His heartfelt feelings echoed those of several other villagers.

Like Wang Dejun, "living the same life as city dwellers live" is the greatest dream of many villagers. Since this dream was realized in 2019, about 35,000 residents have been enjoying their new homes in the Zhengzhou Airport Economy Zone. Like Wang Dejun's family, these residents all started new lives in the well-located modern community with convenient transportation and perfect amenities, and celebrated a jubilant Chinese New Year in their new homes.

Unprecedented challenges and opportunities come hand-in-hand with each other. How can an unknown rural town be turned into a new modern metropolis?

安置居民回迁后的幸福生活
The Happy Lives of Resettled Residents

弹指一挥间,航空港实验区踩着新型城镇化的鼓点迅猛成长,从蹒跚学步到风华正茂,一路追梦高歌猛进,一路跨越势不可挡。截至2020年底,航空港实验区安置房累计9.26万套,让数十万回迁百姓对于美好生活的期待变为鲜活的生活场景。

伴随着新型城镇化的春风,一同拔地而起的还有一座座商业综合体、写字楼、特色商业等多种业态,共同构建起了这座新兴城市的雏形。豫发、正弘、永威、万科等多家河南省知名企业以及全国地产知名企业项目开始落地这座新兴的城市,以新郑国际机场、富士康为中心,一路延

How can villagers be transformed into urbanites?

The answer is all-in-one urbanization. As China's first aviation economy pilot zone approved by the State Council, the Zhengzhou Airport Economy Zone is both a trial and a demonstration of new urban construction. The strategy of "all-in-one urbanization" was put forward at the beginning of the construction of the Zhengzhou Airport Economy Zone based on the principle of being people-oriented, and it aimed from the beginning to accelerate the renovation of shantytowns and to create a new urban space that is "habitable and business-friendly" through the construction of high-quality modern communities.

As if with a flick of a finger, the Zhengzhou Airport Economy Zone grew rapidly with the progress of new urbanization. Great strides were made in an unstoppable way to build the Zhengzhou Airport Economy Zone from scratch. By the end of 2020, there were 92,600 resettlement houses in the Zhengzhou Airport Economy Zone, and hundreds of thousands of relocated people started happy new lives.

河东安置区及配套中学
Hedong Resettlement Community and Its Affiliated Middle School

With the development of new urbanization, commercial complexes, office buildings, and businesses have sprung up together to build the foundation of this emerging city. This emerging city is home to many enterprises that are well known

展、多点开花,逐渐填充着这座城市的骨架。

"简直不敢相信这是短短几年间发生的变化,刚来的时候还是一片沙土地,通往市区的道路还只有华夏大道。"回头看着自己身后的土地发生的巨变,李俊生很庆幸自己当初选择了航空港实验区,选择了在这片土地上成家立业。对未来,李俊生也充满了期待,"希望下一个7年,航空港区会越来越好"。

新家里的幸福新生活
Happy New Life in the Resettlement Houses

初生的航空新城正在规划建设者的"魔法棒"下一步步完成它的"蝶变",但规划者们也深知,"全域城镇化"不是简单地盖高楼,修大路,也不是单指平房变楼房,农民变市民。就业,才是民生之本。

因此,在建设之初,航空港实验区就提出了"以产兴城、产城融合"的发展道路。智能终端、临空生物医药、郑州合晶硅、华锐光电等一系列战略性新兴产业、龙头企业的培育和落地投产,更是为周边居民在家门口铺好了就业致富的"康庄大道"。

High-rise Buildings around Kangping Lake Park

in Henan Province, such as Yufa, Zhenghong, Youwell and Vanke, as well as real estate projects that are well known in China. With the Xinzheng International Airport and Foxconn as the anchors, a clear structure of the city has been formed.

"I can't believe all of this has been developed in just a few years. When I first came here, this was nothing but a piece of sandy land, and the only road leading to the city was Huaxia Avenue." Looking back at the great changes to the area, Li Junsheng is very glad that he chose to settle down in the Zhengzhou Airport Economy Zone. He is also looking forward to the future. "I hope that the

6 点整，家住王家庄村的王丽新就开始利落地打扫屋子，准备一家人的早饭……之所以比以往提前半个小时起床，是因为她在家门口找到了合适的工作，成了航空港实验区智能终端（手机）产业园酷美智能科技有限公司的一名正式员工。

"在家附近工作，既能增加家庭收入，也能照顾到家里的一双小儿女。"王丽新喜滋滋地说，"挣钱、顾家两不误"。

上午 8 点半，王丽新准时来到了智能终端（手机）产业园。环顾四周，一栋栋充满现代气息和工业美感的厂房错落有致，"智能终端（手机）产业园"的牌匾在阳光的映射下熠熠生辉。"在这儿上班真是得劲！"王丽新忍不住地感慨。

谁也无法想象，多年前，这里还是一片片枣林田地；如今，这里已是备受瞩目的重要手机制造基地，富士康、中兴、酷派、创维等智能终端相关企业相继签约入驻，扛起了推进航空港实验区制造业向中高端迈进的大旗，也带动数万居民在此就业。

新兴产业带动就业，只是航空港实验区搭好"就业桥"、铺好"致富路"的一个方面，各类层出不穷的大型招聘会也是扩大就业的"法宝"。

2019 年 3 月，航空港实验区"春风行动"专场招聘会顺利举行，来自区内外的近百家用人单位，包括富士康、中国太平洋保险、花花牛乳业、航空港实验区智能终端（手机）产业园等在内的重点企业携 2000 多个岗位参与了这次招聘。"这项招聘活动近几年我们每年都办，今年现场达成初步就业意向的就高达 300 余人。"航空港实验区人社局相关负责人颇有感慨地介绍到。

除了实施公共就业服务专项活动，航空港实验区还大力推进全民职业技能提升工程，由各办事处联合区内企业，针对失地农民定向开展职业技能培训，巡防队员、育林绿化、物业服务、汽车维修……一个个未曾听闻的新名词慢慢走进寻常百姓家，成为回迁居民养家糊口的新技能。

Zhengzhou Airport Economy Zone will get better and better over the next seven years."

The newborn aviation town is transforming dramatically with planning and construction, but planners also know that "all-in-one urbanization" is not simply about high-rise buildings and road repair, nor does it simply mean changing bungalows into high-rise buildings and farmers into urbanites. Employment is the foundation of people's livelihoods.

Therefore, prior to the construction, the Zhengzhou Airport Economy Zone put forward the development plan of "integrating industries with the city". The cultivation of a series of strategic emerging industries and leading enterprises, such as intelligent terminals, Life Zhengzhou Park, Wafer Works (Zhengzhou) Corp. and Huarui Optoelectronics, have paved a "broad road" for the surrounding residents to be employed at their doorsteps.

华锐光电厂房内景
The Inside View of Huarui Optoelectronics

At 6 o'clock sharp, Wang Lixin, who lives in Wangjiazhuang Village, began to clean the house and prepare breakfast for her family. The reason why she got up half an hour earlier than before was that she has found herself a suitable job at her doorstep and become a full-time employee of Kumei Intelligent Technology Co.,

中部人力资源产业园
The Central China Human Resources Industrial Park

更令人欣喜的是，2019年11月，位于华夏大道旁的中部人力资源产业园正式开园，省社保中心、人才交流中心、公共就业服务中心等12家省人社厅公共服务机构入驻园区。园区的共享招聘大厅里，现代化招聘展位轮番播放着企业宣传片。未来，这里有望成为航空港实验区新的"人气"核心。

"好日子更有盼头了！"王丽新信心满满地说道。是的，对于航空港实验区的新市民来说，美好生活不仅是新家靓起来、社区美起来，更

How can the growing needs of the people in the region for better lives be met while ensuring employment and stabilizing people's livelihoods? Facing an ever-growing population, the planners and builders of the Zhengzhou Airport Economy Zone have been thinking about this question constantly. It didn't take long for them to find the answer. In June, 2015, Zhengzhou issued *The Guiding Opinions on The Planning and Construction of Zhengzhou's "Three Levels and Three Types" Citizen Service Centers*, which put forward detailed requirements on the guiding ideology, construction principles, construction content and implementation measures of the convenience service center projects. This broadened the mind of builders of the Zhengzhou Airport Economy Zone and pointed out the direction for the construction of convenience service centers.

Taking advantage of Zhengzhou's guidance with regard to the construction of citizen service centers, the Zhengzhou Airport Economy Zone went all out to build a "fifteen-minute convenient living circle", planning to build twenty-three convenience service centers and naming them "neighborhood centers". "Harmony makes the neighborhood and cordial integration creates harmony," that is, we hope to realize harmonious and healthy neighborhood relations. Therefore, the "one-stop intelligent life service platform" with the aim of assisting and benefiting people was officially launched in the Zhengzhou Airport Economy Zone, and opened a new chapter in intelligent life services.

On May 6, 2020, the Liaison Station of the People's Congress Working Committee of the Neighborhood Center Cihang Road Service Center and the Command Center of the Zhengzhou Airport Economy Zone were successfully renovated and opened. The two centers are striving to become the pilot and demonstration areas at the grassroots level of Alibaba's big data technology.

On July 17, 2020, Dennis Supermarket opened for business in a neighborhood center on Chang'an Road, and was packed with shoppers that day. "Dennis is a familiar brand in Zhengzhou. Its shopping centers are not only clean, spacious and bright, but also provide many kinds of goods and good service." Having learned that Dennis Supermarket was about to open, Li Yi'an, who lived in Jinxiu Cuiyuan, arrived at the door to the Dennis Supermarket well before 8: 00 am. "It only takes me five minutes to walk to this supermarket. It's really convenient to have a large shopping center at my doorstep. I feel really good about this." Li Yi'an nodded and

业区带来的生活便利，李意安连连点头称赞。

对普通市民来说，邻里中心给他们最直观的感受就是以家为中心，1千米范围内便能找到各类生活服务场所，步行10—15分钟就能将生活打理得井井有条。事实上，邻里中心能提供的服务远不止这些，几乎涵盖了日常生活中的所有需求，从"柴米油盐酱醋茶"到"衣食住行闲"都有所涉及，为社区居民提供"一站式"社区服务。与一般商业中心不同的是，邻里中心的业态配比以服务业为主导，菜市场、餐饮店、超市、美容美发店、家政服务、药店、银行、邮政、卫生所等与居民日常生活息息相关的为必备业态。

这样，居民只要走进邻里中心，就可以买菜、吃饭、洗衣、理发等，甚至连修拉链、配钥匙这样的琐碎需求也可完成，真正实现一站式满足"柴米油盐酱醋茶，衣食住行闲"等基本生活需求。简而言之，就是你日常生活所需要的服务，买菜做饭、家政养老、锻炼购物，邻里中心都能全方位提供。

"以后不用开车就能去逛商场了，不仅生活、购物和办事更加方便，而且也多了一个增强邻里情感的好去处。"家住锦绣翠园小区的老李对

美丽校园

A Beautiful Campus

居民生活日益便利
Residents' lives are becoming more and more convenient.

praised the convenience brought by this neighborhood center.

For ordinary citizens, the neighborhood center makes it possible for them to find all kinds of service within one kilometer from their home, and everything in their daily lives can be taken care of within a ten-to-fifteen-minute walk. In fact, the neighborhood centers can provide far more services than those that have already been mentioned. All the needs of daily life, from daily necessities like woods, rice, oil, salt, soy sauce, vinegar and tea to food, clothing, housing, transportation and leisure activities, can be provided by the one-stop community services. Different from ordinary commercial centers, neighborhood centers are service industry-oriented; therefore, wet markets, restaurants, supermarkets, beauty salons, housekeeping services, pharmacies, banks, postal services, health centers and other stores closely related to residents' daily lives are gathered here.

Residents can buy vegetables, have meals, wash their clothes, and get their hair cut simply by walking to the neighborhood center. Even small errands like repairing zippers and copying keys can be done at the neighborhood center, thus truly realizing the goal of having all of people's basic needs satisfied in one-stop shopping. In short, neighborhood centers can provide all-round services to meet residents' needs in their daily lives, such as buying food and cooking, housekeeping and taking care of the elderly, and exercising and shopping.

"I can go shopping without having to drive, which is more convenient for me, and it also provides a good place to bump into and get to know my neighbors."

于郑港第二便民中心的开业运营表示期待，"娃儿的幼儿园在小区里，小学就在社区旁边，现在又有了逛街、休闲的地方，生活啊，是越来越得劲儿了"。

更让人欣喜的是，随着航空港实验区的快速发展，来自全球的货物在新郑国际机场分拨至全国各地，跨境电商的快速发展、进口免税店的设立，航空港实验区的新市民开始与世界同步，轻松便捷购买心仪的进口商品。荷兰的鲜花、澳洲的牛肉、墨西哥的牛油果……如今，在航空港实验区跨境电商免税店便可"一站式"购齐，这些昔日的"稀罕物"也越来越频繁出现在中原百姓的生活中。

"想买一些进口的商品，再也不用费心海淘找代购了，自己在家门口就能够购买，非常方便，而且价格也不贵。"在空港跨境免税店，已经在航空港实验区安家的市民王先生购买了德国啤酒以及俄罗斯提拉米苏、果汁后表示。

在繁忙的工作之余，不失邻里亲情，还能随时随地享受便利生活的乐趣，或许，这便是惬意而居之所在。

城市的理想生活状态，是看得见的高品质生活，不仅享有城市的繁华生活，更诠释着人们自然栖居的梦想。当镜头对准航空港实验区，双鹤湖中央公园、郑州园博园以及苑陵故城遗址公园格外惹眼，三座园子"承包"了航空港实验区的大部分"颜值"，给这里带来勃勃生机。

"我家就在公园旁，吃过饭就能和家人来公园里遛个弯儿，感受那微风拂面、蝉鸣耳畔的亲水浪漫。"对于工作于此的王佳佳来说，周末的午后，和家人一起漫步于双鹤湖中央公园，是一天中最惬意的时光。

双鹤湖中央公园，命名源自河南新郑"郑公大墓"出土的春秋中期青铜水器——莲鹤方壶，是一座以"莲鹤方壶"的"鹤"为核心设计理念的城市中央公园。莲鹤方壶装饰异常瑰丽繁复，风格集奇诡与清新于一身，是春秋时期青铜艺术的代表之作。这产于春秋年间的"新郑彝器"，不仅是国之重宝，也为双鹤湖中央公园提供了创意起点和精神内核。

Grandpa Li, who lives in Jinxiu Cuiyuan Community, is looking forward to the opening of Zhenggang No.2 Convenience Center. "My grandchild's preschool is in the neighborhood, and the primary school is next to the residential community. Now there is a place to go shopping and relax. Life is truly getting better and better."

What is even more gratifying is that with the rapid development of the Zhengzhou Airport Economy Zone, goods from all over the world are distributed to all parts of the country from Xinzheng International Airport. With the rapid development of cross-border e-commerce and the establishment of duty-free shops, new denizens of the Zhengzhou Airport Economy Zone have begun to keep pace with the world and can easily purchase their favorite imported goods. Flowers from Holland, beef from Australia, avocados from Mexico, goods that were rarely seen in the Central Plains in the past, now can be purchased in one stop at the cross-border e-commerce duty-free shops in the Zhengzhou Airport Economy Zone.

"If you want to buy some imported goods, you don't have to bother to find a purchasing agent any more. You can buy them at your doorstep, which is convenient and inexpensive." Mr. Wang, who has settled down in the Zhengzhou Airport Economy Zone, said after buying German beer, Russian tiramisu and juice in the airport cross-border duty-free shop.

After a hard day's work, without ever leaving the warmth of the neighborhood, you can enjoy this convenient life's pleasure anytime and anywhere. Perhaps, this is what we call a pleasant living experience.

For a city, the ideal state of life is to produce a visibly high-quality life, to allow the enjoyment of flourishing life, as well as to truly give voice to people's spontaneous dreams. Shuanghe (two cranes) Lake Central Park, Zhengzhou Expo Garden and Yuanling Ancient City Site are particularly eye-catching places in the Zhengzhou Airport Economy Zone. These three sites are the calling cards of the Zhengzhou Airport Economy Zone and bring great vitality to it.

"My home is next to the park. After dinner, I can walk around the park with my family and feel the romance in the breeze and in the chirping of cicadas." For Wang Jiajia, who works here, walking with his family in Shuanghe Lake Central Park on a weekend afternoon is the most pleasant activity of the day.

第三章 航空大都市

秀美航空港
The Exquisitely Beautiful Zhengzhou Airport Economy Zone

结合水体、地形等展开规划设计，双鹤湖中央公园将"鹤"的元素贯穿到园区细节设计中——桥梁、灯柱、步道、喷泉……摹其形、拟其态，新兴现代文明科技碰撞传统文化气韵。将园区独有的文化、景色与时下热点结合，赏其韵、传其神，郑州首家定向运动主题公园正式落户

Shuanghe Lake Central Park is named after Lianhe (lotus and crane) Square Pot, a bronze water vessel cast during the middle of the Spring and Autumn Period that was unearthed from Zhenggong Tomb in Xinzheng, Henan Province. The park is in the center of the city, and is shaped like a crane. The decoration of the Lianhe Square Pot is extremely magnificent and intricate, and its style combines uniqueness and freshness. It is an emblematic work of bronze art from the Spring and Autumn Period. This "Xinzheng Ritual Bronzeware" produced during the Spring and Autumn Period not only is a national treasure, but also provides the creative starting point and spiritual core for the design of Shuanghe Lake Central Park.

双鹤湖中央公园鸟瞰图
An Aerial View of Shuanghe Lake Central Park

于此。"能在美景中体验精彩纷呈的定向运动，寻找自我、熔炼团队，是一件十分畅快的事儿。"定向比赛结束后，队员王贺丽仍意犹未尽。

走出双鹤湖中央公园，沿着梁州大道，驾车十余分钟便抵达了郑州园博园。若摊开地图，便会发现一柄"绿如意"跃然而出。郑州园博园便位于"如意"的一端。

2017年9月，以"传承华夏文明、引领绿色发展"为主题的第十一届中国（郑州）国际园林博览会在此举行，园博会后，郑州园博园作为综合性城市公园永久保留，持续发挥生态惠民功能。皇家园林的大气恢宏、苏州园林的婉约诗意、江南坞馆的温婉细腻、西域建筑的豪迈奔放……园中汇聚东西南北园林精髓，尽显华夏特色，堪称一座现代建筑艺术与古典文化的交融之园。

施施而行，漫漫而游，园林各异，水木清华。"夕阳的余晖洒在湖面上，泛着点点波光，让这个值得纪念的日子更显浪漫。"同心湖畔，一对新人正在拍摄婚纱照，如果可以，他们想把婚礼也放在这里举办。

"如意"的另一端便是苑陵故城遗址公园。它与郑州园博园分居两端遥相呼应，一古一今，象征着历史文化的传承与发展。以古遗址保护为前提、以展示秦汉农耕文明为主线，苑陵故城遗址公园打造"六圃九囿景观"，再现农耕时代生产生活场景。营造花林草地、花卉长廊、花耕农田，渲染故城秋之绚烂、冬之苍翠、春之明媚、夏之斑斓的四季景色，还原一城生机盎然的"苑陵群芳圃"。

相比公园，苑陵故城更是一本活史书，一砖一瓦都镌刻着历史。据文献记载，商王武丁曾封其子文于苑（即苑陵）为侯爵，世称苑侯，这便是苑陵故城的发端。到了西周时期，这里则极可能是郐国的都城。正如《括地志》记载："故郐城在郑州新郑县东北三十二里。"郑樵《通志》中也提到："今新郑县东北三十五里有古郐城是也。"和历史并行的苑陵故城，走过了千载。由此诞生的"苑"姓，也在华夏大地生生不息地流传繁衍。

Elements of crane were incorporated into the detailed planning and design of Shuanghe Lake Central Park. The bridges, lampposts, trails, and fountains all adopt the crane's shape or imitate its posture, an example of the combination of emerging modern technology with the charm of traditional culture. Combining the unique culture and scenery of the park with current trends, the first orienteering theme park in Zhengzhou has officially settled here. "It is really nice to experience orienteering activities, find yourself and build team spirit in the beautiful scenery." After the orienteering competition, Wang Heli was still excited.

Walking out of Shuanghe Lake Central Park and driving along Liangzhou Avenue, it takes only a little more than ten minutes to arrive at Zhengzhou Expo

百花争艳映园博
Flowers in Zhengzhou Expo Garden Park

正弘中央公园水天一色
Breathtaking Scenery in Zhenghong Central Park

"咔嚓",已有上千年历史的苑陵古城墙定格在游人的镜头里。"这里有皇家出宫祭祀的威仪,也有市井生活的淡淡烟火,这里的一砖一瓦都承载着历史的沧桑与厚重。"

植根于深厚底蕴的航空港实验区,"旧"与"新"和谐并存,"古"与"今"相得益彰。漫步航空新城,如同走入一幅绿色的画卷中。除了秀美"三园",康平湖公园、梅河公园、兰河公园、恩平湖公园等综合性公园也如"大珠小珠落玉盘"似的散落在航空港实验区南北,南水北

Garden Park. If you spread out the map, a grand green Ruyi-shaped [1] park will jump out at you. Zhengzhou Expo Garden Park is located at one end of this Ruyi.

In September 2017, the 11th China (Zhengzhou) International Garden Expo with the theme of "Inheriting Chinese Civilization and Leading Green Development" was held here. After the exposition, Zhengzhou Expo Garden Park was permanently preserved as a comprehensive city park and will continue to bring ecological benefits to local residents. You may find the essence of all the different types of Chinese gardens here, including the grand atmosphere of imperial gardens, the graceful and reserved poetic ambience of Suzhou gardens, the gentle and delicate Yangtze Delta gardens, and the heroic and magnificent

苑陵故城遗址公园秋色醉人
Mesmerizing Autumn Scenery in Yuanling Ancient City Site Park

---

[1] Ruyi is a traditional Chinese artefact symbolizing auspiciousness. It is often made of jade, bamboo or bones, with a cloud-shaped head and a curved handle.

华夏大道绿意盎然
Vibrant Plants along Huaxia Avenue

调干渠更是如同一架巨大的拱桥,在航空港实验区划过27千米长的弯弧,守护着这座城市的"绿色梦想"。

"现在环境跟着生活一起美起来,每天就想沿着家门口的公园多走走转转。"家住航空港实验区正弘中央公园的王宏丰老人虽年逾七十,但身板硬朗,说起话来中气十足,"现在一到傍晚,公园里休闲散步的人可多了,也给我们老年人提供了休闲娱乐的空间"。

除了散落在航空港实验区南北大大小小的公园,600多万平方米的

architecture of gardens in the Western Regions in ancient China. It is truly a garden park where classical culture and modern architecture blend together.

You may revel in all kinds of gardens here during a leisurely walk. "The afterglow of the sunset sparkle on the lake, glowing with the waves, which makes this memorable day even more romantic." On Tongxin Lake, a newlywed couple is taking wedding photos. They also wish to have their wedding ceremony here.

At the other end of the Ruyi is Yuanling Ancient City Site Park. It mirrors Zhengzhou Expo Garden Park on the other end, one from ancient times and the other from the present, symbolizing the inheritance and development of history and culture respectively. With the protection of the ancient site in mind, Yuanling Ancient City Site Park has been divided into six gardens and nine hunting areas to reproduce working and living scenes far back in the farming era in order to display the farming civilization of the Qin and Han dynasties. Flowers and grasslands have been cultivated here to bring back the seasonal scenery of the old city and to represent the vibrant "Yuanling Flowers Garden."

Compared to a typical park, Yuanling Ancient City Site is a living history book, with traces of history easily found everywhere. According to historical records, King Wuding of the Shang Dynasty once named his son Lord Wen of Yuan (Yuanling), so Wen became known as Yuanhou. This was the beginning of the Yuanling Ancient City Site. In the Western Zhou Dynasty, Yuanling was most likely the capital of the state of Kuai. As recorded in *Kuo Di Zhi* (a book on the history of the administrative divisions of the Tang Dynasty), "The previous Kuai city was located thirty-two *li* (1 *li* ≈ 0.31 mile) northeast of Zhengzhou's Xinzheng county." Zheng Qiao's *Tongzhi* (historical records written during the Southern Song Dynasty) also mentioned that, "The previous Kuai city was located thirty-five *li* northeast of Zhengzhou's Xinzheng county." The Yuanling Ancient City Site has passed through thousands of years of history. The surname "Yuan", which was born here, has been inherited in China by generation after generation.

With the click of a shutter, the ancient city wall of Yuanling, which has a history of thousands of years, is captured in time in the cameras of tourists. "Here you will find the dignity of royal ceremonies and an earthly living atmosphere. Every nook and cranny of the site bears witness to the magnitude of history."

In the Zhengzhou Airport Economy Zone, the old and the new coexist

林、水、城相互交织，人与自然和谐共处
The Interwoven Presence of Trees, Water and the City Echoes the Harmonious Coexistence of Human Beings and Nature

生态廊道和条条景观带如珠链串起个个游园，辉映在生机盎然的大地上。行走其间"300米见绿、500米见园"，真正实现了"林、水、城相互交融，人与自然和谐共生"，让人不由得叹一声："景湖相连、景水相依，城在山水间，人在画中游。"绿色正在融入城市血脉，成为这座新城的城市底色和发展主色。

harmoniously, and antiquity and the present complement each other. Walking through the new aviation city is like walking into a scene from a green ink painting on a scroll. In addition to the exquisite three parks mentioned above, Kangping Lake Park, Meihe Park, Lanhe Park and Enping Lake Park and other parks are scattered like a string of pearls onto a jade plate in the north and south parts of the Zhengzhou Airport Economy Zone. The main canal of the South-to-North Water Diversion Project is like a huge arch bridge, stretching over a range of twenty-seven kilometers in the Zhengzhou Airport Economy Zone.

"Now the environment is becoming more and more beautiful, just like our lives, and it's a delight to walk around the park just at my doorstep every day." Wang Hongfeng, who lives in Zhenghong Central Park, a community in the Zhengzhou Airport Economy Zone, is over seventy years old, but he is still very healthy and has a resonant voice. "Now in the evening, there are more people than before taking a leisurely walk in the park. It provides a good location for leisure and recreation for elderly people, like me."

In addition to various parks scattered in the north and south parts of the Zhengzhou Airport Economy Zone, more than six million square meters of ecological corridors and landscape belts are connected together like a string of pearls, glowing vibrantly on the land. Anyone who walks in this area can see greenery every three hundred meters and a garden every five hundred meters, truly realizing the integration of the forest, the water and the city, along with the harmonious coexistence between people and nature. People are amazed by the blending of scenery and water, and by the blurred boundary between the city and nature. Walking around here is like touring through a landscape painting. Being "green" is merging into the blood of the city and becoming the background color and thematic color of the city's development.

三、智通空港引未来

从工作到生活的距离需要多久才算恰好？30 分钟。在美国孟菲斯地区的复合型社区里，产业依托机场而建，学校、医院、住宅围绕分布，产城融合构建起 30 分钟生活圈。

在"购物天堂"阿联酋迪拜，机场内 9000 平方米的免税店 24 小时开门迎客，来自世界各地的商品琳琅满目，临空经济拓展城郊商业新版图。

有着"盒子里的城市"之称的韩国松岛新城，被看成是全球智慧城市的模板。在这里，远程呈现设备像洗碗机一样普遍，用户能够远程接受教育、医疗和公共福利，开启"指尖上的生活"。

21 世纪，国际枢纽机场正成为驱动城市发展的重要因素，依托综合航空运输体系迅速崛起的航空都市将成为城市化的新模式，是全球城市的未来。在中国，航空港实验区因其独有优势，正逐步成为航空都市建设的引领者。

未来，这片土地上的人们将如何生活？

乘车出门，一路绿灯。这不是运气，而是智慧型路口的"杰作"。信号灯杆上的微波检测仪好似"眼睛"，实时调整红绿灯频率，有效避免不必要的拥堵。

政务服务，越来越多政务部门、职能机构的"办事大厅"，从线下"复制"到线上，处理事务只需指尖轻点。

紧急救援，智慧系统通过对灾情进行分析，计算周边交通及路况，将警报分发给距离最近的消防、公安、卫生等协同部门，并给出最佳救援方案……

这不是想象，而是航空港实验区正在逐步普及的现实场景。早在 2017 年，航空港实验区便提出要建设"智慧人文宜居航空大都市"。

III. A Smart Airport Embraces the Future

What is the ideal time of the commute from work to life? Thirty minutes. In the neighborhoods near the airport in Memphis in the United States, all the industries are airport-based. Schools, hospitals and residential areas are distributed around the airport, creating a thirty-minute living circle.

In the "shopping paradise" of Dubai in the United Arab Emirates, the nine-thousand-square-meter duty-free shop in the airport is open twenty-four hours a day, seven days a week to provide a wide variety of goods from all over the world. Here the airport economy drives the development of suburban commerce.

New Songdo City, South Korea, known as the "city in the box", is regarded as a template for smart cities around the world. Here, remote devices are as common as dishwashers. Remote access to education, medical care and public welfare are at users' fingertips.

In the 21st century, the international airport hub is becoming an important driving force for the development of cities. The rapidly rising aviation city, relying on the comprehensive air transport system, will become a new mode of urbanization and a pattern for future global cities. In China, due to its unique advantages, the Zhengzhou Airport Economy Zone is gradually becoming a model that aviation cities of the future will be able to copy.

How do people in the Zhengzhou Airport Economy Zone live in the future?

When people are driving on the street, all the traffic lights ahead are green. This may not be pure luck, but rather a "masterpiece" of intelligent intersections. The microwave detectors on the traffic light poles are like "eyes", which adjust the frequency of traffic lights in real time and effectively avoid unnecessary congestion.

More and more service halls of government departments and organizations are "copied" from offline to online, and relevant affairs can be taken care of with a few clicks of a mouse.

Intelligent systems can analyze the status of disasters, calculate surrounding traffic and road conditions, and send an alarm to the nearest fire station, public security department, health department and other relevant departments, so as to

时至今日，系列智慧项目已在航空港实验区落地开花，"智慧"无处不在，"智慧生活"也正在成为每个航空港实验区居民的生活常态。

智慧生活，触手可及
Accessible Intelligent Life

provide the best rescue plan under the conditions.

This is not wild imagination, but scenes that are gradually being realized in the Zhengzhou Airport Economy Zone. Even as early as 2017, the planners of the Zhengzhou Airport Economy Zone had proposed building a "smart, humanistic and habitable aviation metropolis". Now, a series of smart projects have been launched in the Zhengzhou Airport Economy Zone, "intelligence" is everywhere, and "intelligent life" is becoming the normal life of every resident in the zone.

Besides giving off light, what is the function of street lamps? "Intelligent lamp poles can do whatever you wish them to do!" some people once said. Indeed, in the Zhengzhou Airport Economy Zone, lighting is currently only the most basic function of the street lamps. In the zone, each of the 3,996 street lamps has its own "ID card" that indicates all kinds of information such as serial number, coordinates, location, ownership and administrative region. With the "ID card", the street lamp information can be published on an electronic map, and a geographic information system of the city's lighting can be established. Based on this information, the location of the street lamp can be located, and the real-time status of the street lamp can be grasped, so quick positioning and response can be undertaken when any street lamp fails. Sharing street lamp information with the municipal departments can also support more applications, such as sharing data with the public security system, and using lamp pole numbers as a positioning reference for public security emergency calls and urban emergency response.

Smart prosecutorial work integrates remote arraignment, remote tripartite court sessions, reception of litigants, and summoning criminal suspects into the intelligent judicial casework field, breaking the boundaries of time and space, and conducting the trial of cases without anyone having to leave home. Big data, cloud computing, intelligent interaction and other means will allow students to be taught in accordance with their aptitude. Smart urban management will enable every nook and cranny to go online and finally realize the "scientific, strict, granular and long-term" management of the city. Smart police will be able to see the deployment of their forces clearly at a glance on the three-dimensional visual map, moving away from "sweat policing" to "smart policing" . The implementation of a series of smart projects has improved people's livelihoods bit by bit. Yet this is only the beginning

路灯除了照明，还有什么作用？"只有你们想不到的，没有智慧灯杆做不到的！"曾有人这样说。的确，在当前的航空港实验区，照明仅仅是路灯最基础最底层的功能。在这里，3996杆路灯拥有着自己的"身份证"，编号、坐标、位置、权属和行政区域信息一应俱全。有了"身份证"，就可以将这些路灯信息发布于电子地图中，建立城市照明地理信息系统，基于这些信息实现对路灯的位置定位，掌握路灯的实时状态，从而在路灯出现故障时做到快速定位、响应。将路灯信息与市政平台进行数据共享，还可支持更多应用，如与公安系统数据联通，可将灯杆编号作为110报警、城市应急指挥的定位参照。

智慧检务将远程提讯、远程三方开庭、接待当事人、传唤犯罪嫌疑人等工作统一纳入智能化司法办案工作区，打破时空界限，实现"足不出户"就能审理案件；依靠大数据、云计算、智能交互等手段，开启教育"智慧密码"，实现因材施教的个性化教学；智慧城管让城市的每一个单元、每一个因子"上线"联网，最终实现对城市的"科学、严格、精细、长效"管理；智慧公安实现警力部署在三维可视地图一目了然，从而实现由"汗水警务"向"智慧警务"迈进……系列智慧项目的落地生根，一点一滴改善着这座城市的民生感知，而这只是航空港实验区智慧城市建设的开端。

要让城市像人一样具备"思考力"，就要搭建起一个个"器官"，赋予它思考的能力。"数据大脑"——数据中心，"千里之眼"——地理信息云平台，"神经系统"——高速通信网作为智慧城市重要的"器官"构成，为整个体系构建奠定着坚实的基础。智慧城市数据中心通过对硬件资源和基础数据的整合利用，实现绿色节能、信息共享及业务协同，促进政务管理、民生服务和产业发展的全面提升；地理信息云平台则以实景模拟方式展现，实现全区基础地理信息统一集聚和数据整合，为城市规划和精细化管理提供基础地理信息服务；而高速通信网则通过安全稳定的通信网络加快航空港实验区智慧化步伐，为智慧城市业务互联互

of smart city construction in the Zhengzhou Airport Economy Zone.

To let cities "think" like people, it's necessary to build "organs" and give them the ability to learn. Data centers are the "brains". The geographic information cloud platform is the "penetrating eyes". The high-speed communication network is the "nervous system". These important "organs" have laid a solid foundation for the construction of the whole system. Through the integration and utilization of hardware resources and basic data, the smart city data center has achieved green energy conservation, information sharing and business collaboration, and has promoted the overall improvement of government management, basic living needs fulfillment, and industrial development. The geographic information cloud platform is displayed in the form of a real-life simulation, resulting in the unified gathering and integration of basic geographic information in the whole region, and providing basic geographic information services for urban planning and granular management. The high-speed communication network accelerates the progress of intelligence in the Zhengzhou Airport Economy Zone through a secure and stable communication network, paving a "highway" for business interconnectivity in the smart city. They are like three pillars, propping up the "temple" of the smart city in the Zhengzhou Airport Economy Zone. A series of smart projects closely related to people's lives are like "capable generals" supported by data centers, geographic information cloud platforms and high-speed communication networks, and are responsible for accurately solving problems in urban development.

June 23, 2020 marked the completion of the in-orbit construction of the third generation Beidou Navigation Satellite System (BDS-3). The Zhengzhou Airport Economy Zone firmly seized this opportunity to follow the national strategy, taking advantage of Beidou to power the development of the Central Plains. The Zhengzhou Airport Economy Zone has begun building Beidou Industrial Park, attracted industry leaders to move to the zone, set up UniStrong (Henan) Science and Technology Research Institute, pooled global resources to promote research and development, and propelled the Zhengzhou Airport Economy Zone to become a world-class positioning, navigation, technology innovation nexus and industrial gathering place. According to the plan, the Zhengzhou Airport Economy Zone and Beidou Industrial Park will develop a "cloud + port" IoT

通铺就"高速公路"。它们犹如三大柱石,撑起了航空港实验区智慧城市建设的"神殿",和人们生活息息相关的系列智慧项目,则是依托数据中心、地理信息云平台与高速通信网培养出来的"良将","点对点"解决城市发展的痛点。

2020年6月23日,北斗三号全球组网收官。在智慧之路探索前行的航空港实验区紧紧抓住这一契机,紧随国家战略,借势北斗赋能中原。建设北斗产业园,吸引产业龙头落户,成立合众思壮(河南)科技研究院,整合全球资源推动研发,助推航空港实验区成为世界级定位导航及时空技术的创新高地和产业聚集地。根据规划,双方将以航空港实验区智慧城市应用需求为基础,发展"云+端"时空物联应用示范区,形成智慧城市和智慧行业的典型应用,引领智慧发展。

当下,一个个落地的项目如繁花簇锦。未来,一项项智慧规划也将如雨后春笋般呈现,航空港实验区仿佛具备了智慧,会思考、会规划……服务着这片土地上每一个息息相关的个体。

科技的发展如影随形,与城市共演进,默默地改变着城市的样貌,牵动着我们的生活。而推动这一切的关键要素,便是人。"在引进专家时,我们会因人而异制定政策,灵活安排工作时间,一对一服务,等等。这种柔性机制确保了专家为航空港实验区发展做出实际的工作,真正发挥其应有作用。"时任航空港实验区人社局局长周英聊到,"事实上,通过与约翰·卡萨达的合作,我们也在摸索更符合实际、更能发挥人才价值的工作模式,期望能通过实践找到规律性的东西运用到今后的人才引进工作中去,让'外脑'真正为航空港实验区开放型经济发展支招"。正如上文所说,航空港实验区成立之初便十分重视人才工作,在人才引进上下足了功夫。

在航空港实验区获批的第二年,美国北卡罗来纳大学教堂山分校终身荣誉教授、"全球航空经济第一人"、航空都市理论模型创立者约翰·卡萨达就被聘任为首席顾问。而随着航都院正式投入运转,他不仅为航空

(Internet of Things) demonstration zone based on the practical needs of the smart city in the Zhengzhou Airport Economy Zone, building a typical smart city and typical smart industries, thus leading the intelligent development of the area.

Completed projects are now blossoming like flowers. In the future, intelligent plans will spring up like mushrooms. The Zhengzhou Airport Economy Zone will serve everyone in it in a smart way.

The development of science and technology goes hand in hand with that of the city, gradually changing the appearance of the city and people's lives. The key factor behind this development is people. "We have formulated targeted policies to bring in experts, to arrange flexible working hours for them, to provide one-on-one services for them, and to create other favorable conditions for them. This mechanism ensures that experts do practical work for the development of the Zhengzhou Airport Economy Zone and fulfill their duties," said Zhou Ying, then director of the Human Resources and Social Security Bureau of the Zhengzhou Airport Economy Zone. "In fact, through our cooperation with John Kasarda, we are also exploring a work setup that is more realistic and that can give full play to the value of talents. We hope that we can find something regular and apply it to future recruitment, so that the 'invited brain' can truly support the development of the open economy in the Zhengzhou Airport Economy Zone." As mentioned above, the Zhengzhou Airport Economy Zone has attached great importance to the recruitment of top-level talent since its establishment, and great efforts have been made to bring in talented people.

In the year after the Zhengzhou Airport Economy Zone was approved by the State Council, John Kasarda, Professor Emeritus of Aviation Economics at the University of North Carolina at Chapel Hill, the "first pioneer in the global aviation economy" and the founder of the theoretical model of the aviation city, was appointed the Principal Adviser of the Zhengzhou Airport Economy Zone. With the official launch of the Aerotropolis Institute in Zhengzhou, he not only provided strong theoretical guidance for the construction and development of the Zhengzhou Airport Economy Zone, but also spared no effort to promote it. Representatives from international organizations, scholars from famous scientific research institutions, well-known business executives, and industry elites in the field of airport economics from all over the world have been gathered, such

港实验区的建设发展提供了强有力的理论指导，还充分利用其个人在业界的影响力宣传推介航空港实验区，广泛聚集了一批世界各地临空经济领域的国际组织代表、著名科研机构学者、知名企业高管及行业精英，如国际航空货运协会创始人拉姆·梅恩、国际运输与物流专家迈克尔·卡农、北卡罗来纳大学凯南弗拉格勒商学院私营企业研究所企业数字化战略与创新中心主任诺埃尔·格瑞斯，等等，不断凝聚智慧力量，为区域高质量发展提供强有力的人才智力支撑。

2014年，"中国郑州航空港引智试验区"揭牌成立，航空港实验区成为全国第三个国家级引智试验区，正式向世界人才全面开放。这意味着，这里将成为国内外高端专家的聚集地、国际智库基地，吸引更多的世界一流人才和团队，服务航空港实验区的经济发展。随着引智试验区建设的不断推进，为满足海外人才创新创业需求，航空港实验区高标准谋划了海归小镇，以"三园（创新示范园、创新孵化园、新兴产业园）、三区（总部商务区、高层次人才社区、配套服务区）"为空间布局，以科技创新、产业培育、人才培养、产城融合为功能定位，大幅度提高航空港实验区对人才、资本、技术、项目等各类创新资源汇聚和利用的效率、能力和水平，成为航空港实验区导入重大创新资源和人才使用培养的主要平台。

2019年10月26日，第二届中国·河南招才引智创新发展大会和中国·河南开放创新暨跨国技术转移大会在郑州国际会展中心举行，与大会同步开展的还有8场专题论坛、8场主场活动。当日下午，第二届中国·河南招才引智创新发展大会航空港实验区招才引智活动顺利举行，活动共邀请到包括5名海内外院士在内的300余名海内外高层次人才代表参会。其中，最引人注目的一道风景线应属航空港实验区引入的国际智库团队——航空港实验区国际专家委员会，这是河南省首次以"组团式"的方式引入高规格、高水平的国际智库团队，无疑将为航空港实验区打造"中国的航空大都市"提供充沛有力的智力支撑。

as Ram Mayne, founder of the International Air Cargo Association, Michael Cannon, an international transportation and logistics expert; Noel Grace, director of the Center for Enterprise Digital Strategy and Innovation Institute of Private Enterprise, Kennan Flagler Business School, University of North Carolina, etc. These experts have provided strong intellectual support for the high-quality regional development.

In 2014, the "China Zhengzhou Airport Talents Recruitment Experimental Zone" was officially established. The Zhengzhou Airport Economy Zone became the third national talent recruitment experimental zone in the country and was officially opened to talented applicants from all over the world. This means that the Zhengzhou Airport Economy Zone will become a gathering place for top foreign and domestic experts and a center for international think tanks, continuously attracting world-class talent and teams to serve the economic development of the Zhengzhou Airport Economy Zone. With the continuous advancement of the Talents Recruitment Experimental Zone, and in order to meet the innovation and entrepreneurship needs for overseas talent, the Zhengzhou Airport Economy Zone has planned a town reserved for high-level overseas returnees, with "three parks (innovation demonstration park, innovation incubation park and emerging industrial park) and three districts (business headquarters district, high-level talents community district and supporting service district)" as the major parts of the layout, so as to realize the function of scientific and technological innovation, industrial cultivation, personnel cultivation and integration of industry and the city. The purpose is to promote the efficiency, ability and level of gathering and utilizing various innovative resources such as human resources, capital, technology and projects in the Zhengzhou Airport Economy Zone, so as to make the Zhengzhou Airport Economy Zone into a main platform for the introduction of major innovative resources and the use and training of talents in the Zhengzhou Airport Economy Zone.

On October 26, 2019, the Second China Henan Conference on Recruiting and Introducing Talents for Innovation and Development and the Henan Conference on Innovation and Transnational Technology Transfer were held at the Zhengzhou International Convention and Exhibition Center. There were eight other special forums and eight events simultaneously held during the conference.

第二届中国·河南招才引智创新发展大会
The Second China Henan Conference on Recruiting and Introducing Talents for Innovation and Development

"中国的航空大都市——郑州航空港经济综合实验区"品牌也在此正式面向世界发布。"'中国的航空大都市——郑州航空港经济综合实验区'品牌打造是一项系统性工程,将强化航空港实验区作为中国临空经济发展'领头雁'的地位。"约翰·卡萨达表示,"其有助于航空港实验区扩大影响力,向全球展现发展建设的典范形象"。

人才驱动创新,创新驱动发展。如今,航空港实验区航空经济人才高地雏形初步呈现,并已成为海内外人才创新创业的温床、发挥作用的乐土。

That afternoon, the Second Henan Conference on Recruiting and Introducing Talents for Innovation and Development was successfully held in the Zhengzhou Airport Economy Zone. More than 300 high-level talents from China and abroad, including 5 academicians from China and abroad, were invited to attend the event. Among them, the most striking view belonged to the International Experts Committee of the Zhengzhou Airport Economy Zone, the international think tank founded in the Zhengzhou Airport Economy Zone. This was the first time that Henan Province had established a high-level international think tank, which has undoubtedly provided abundant and powerful intellectual support for the Zhengzhou Airport Economy Zone to build "China's Aerotropolis".

"China's Aerotropolis—Zhengzhou Airport Economy Zone" made its debut to the world. "It's a systematic project to make the brand of 'China's Aerotropolis—Zhengzhou Airport Economy Zone, and it will strengthen the Zhengzhou Airport Economy Zone's leading position in China's airport economic development." John Kasarda said, "It will expand the influence of the Zhengzhou Airport Economy Zone and show the world a model for development and construction."

Talent drives innovation and innovation drives development. Nowadays, an aviation economic talent hub in the Zhengzhou Airport Economy Zone has taken shape, and it has become a hotbed for talent from China and from abroad to innovate and start businesses, as well as to make their mark on the world.

结 语

春华秋实，岁物丰成。八年砥砺奋进，航空港实验区加快融入"一带一路"，引领郑州国家中心城市建设，扬起高水平开放龙头，打造河南亮丽名片，谱写了新时代的壮阔篇章。

航空与铁路、公路无缝衔接，多式联运竞相发展，内畅外联、沟通世界的立体交通枢纽加速崛起，这里已成为河南最大的对外开放品牌和带动河南融入全球经济循环的战略平台，连通全球的"空中金桥"正为中原崛起注入强劲动能。

以产业培育"千百亿"工程为牵引，打造新技术、新业态、新模式、新产业创新发展高地，这里已成为先进制造业、现代服务业融合发展的枢纽经济集聚区，产业竞争力不断提升，产业生态圈加快集聚，战略性新兴产业规模持续壮大，在赋能区域经济社会发展的同时，正带动河南产业结构的转型升级。

着眼于未来百万级城市发展需要，加快形成"公共服务中心+机场枢纽+若干功能区"的组团式发展结构。这里已成为产业发达、生态优美、宜居宜业、国际化特征鲜明的航空大都市。汇聚全球智慧，优化营商兴业沃土，人才"强磁场"正释放巨大虹吸效应，创新人才高度集聚，创新成果竞相涌现，创造活力充分并发。

八年奋飞路，今日大都市。展望"十四五"，是航空港实验区加快推进国家中心城市副城高质量建设的关键期，也是贯彻落实国务院批复《郑州航空港经济综合实验区发展规划（2013—2025年）》的收官期。在助力郑州国家中心城市建设、中原更加出彩、中部地区崛起、黄河流域生态保护和高质量发展的新征程上，航空港实验区正扮演着越来越重要的角色，迎来新一轮发展机遇。

Conclusion

Success comes from the unremitting efforts. After eight years of hard work, the Zhengzhou Airport Economy Zone has been fully integrated into the "Belt and Road Initiative", promoted the construction of National Central City, and become a vanguard of reform and opening-up. Now the Zhengzhou Airport Economy Zone is playing a significant part in Henan's economic development.

With seamless connection between air service, railways and highways, as well as the accelerating pace of transportation hub, Zhengzhou Airport Economy Zone has become a window of opening-up and a strategic platform to drive Henan into the global economic cycle. This "Golden Bridge in the Air" connecting the whole world is invigorating the Central Plains.

Guided by the "100 billion and 10 billion" project to cultivate new enterprises (with main operating income exceeding RMB 10 billion to 100 billion), Zhengzhou Airport Economy Zone has become a key economic cluster for the convergence of advanced manufacturing and modern service industries, creating a highland for innovative development of new technologies, new business and new industries. The industrial competitiveness has been continuously improved; the industrial ecological circle has been accelerated; and the scale of strategic emerging industries has continued to grow. While empowering regional economic and social development, the Zhengzhou Airport Economy Zone is driving the transformation and upgrading of Henan's industrial structure.

Focusing on the needs of urban development in the future, Zhengzhou Airport Economy Zone will accelerate the formation of a group development structure of "public service center + airport hub + functional areas". Zhengzhou Airport Economy Zone comes to develop into an aviation metropolis with developed industries, beautiful ecology, habitable surroundings and distinctive international characteristics. By recruiting talented personnel and optimizing business environment, Zhengzhou Airport Economy Zone is becoming increasingly appealing, with innovative talents highly concentrated, innovative achievements competing to emerge, and creativity fully stimulated.

《郑州航空港经济综合实验区条例》自2021年3月1日起施行,明确航空港实验区应当坚持创新、协调、绿色、开放、共享的发展理念,突出国家确定的发展定位,遵循区域统筹、整体规划、协调推进、政府主导、市场运作的原则,积极融入"双循环"新发展格局,实现经济、社会、环境的高质量发展。

河南省委书记王国生对航空港实验区寄予厚望。他指出,要对航空港实验区的重要地位和带动作用再认识再提升,以更多的创新性举措,推动航空港实验区在高质量轨道上健康发展,让这张名片更加亮丽。

河南省委常委、郑州市委书记徐立毅多次到航空港实验区调研督导,提出航空港实验区要紧扣"南动"功能布局,坚持规划引领,加强统筹协调,一体谋划推进开发建设,着力打造对外开放高地,在加快国家中心城市建设、形成更高水平的高质量发展区域增长极中,发挥作用、提供支撑。

2020年11月,航空港实验区召开全区领导干部大会,宣布省委关于航空港实验区党工委、管委会主要领导调整的决定。张俊峰同志任郑州航空港经济综合实验区(郑州新郑综合保税区)党工委书记,万正峰同志任郑州航空港经济综合实验区(郑州新郑综合保税区)党工委副书记、管委会主任。接过沉甸甸的"接力棒",亦是接过了擘画蓝图的如椽巨笔,一幅"交通大枢纽、开放大门户、航空大都市"的宏伟画卷已徐徐铺展,对未来的美好愿景,正化为脚踏实地的生动实践。

鲲鹏展翅,扶摇而上。奋飞的航空港实验区,以"争分夺秒、拼尽

Eight years of hard work brings about today's metropolis. The "14th Five-Year Plan" is the key period for Zhengzhou Airport Economy Zone to accelerate the high-quality construction of the National Central City, and also the final period for implementing *The Development Planning of the Zhengzhou Airport Economy Zone (2013-2025)* approved by the State Council. In the new journey of facilitating Zhengzhou to implement the resolution of constructing National Central City and more brilliant Central Plains, and promoting ecological protection and high-quality development of the Yellow River Basin, Zhengzhou Airport Economy Zone is playing an increasingly important role and welcoming a new round of development opportunities.

The Regulations of Zhengzhou Airport Economy Zone has come into force on March 1, 2021. It is clear that Zhengzhou Airport Economy Zone should adhere to the development concept of innovation, coordination, green, openness and sharing, highlight the development orientation determined by the central government. It will also follow the principles of regional overall planning, coordinated promotion, government-led and market operation, and actively integrate into the new development pattern of "double circulation" to achieve high-quality economic, social and environmental development.

Wang Guosheng, Secretary of the Henan Provincial Party Committee, pinned his hopes on Zhengzhou Airport Economy Zone. On November 27, 2018, when Wang Guosheng went to Zhengzhou Airport Economy Zone for investigation, he stressed that it was essential to have consciousness of the leading role of Zhengzhou Airport Economy Zone, and that more innovative measures should be taken to promote the healthy development of Zhengzhou Airport Economy Zone.

Xu Liyi, member of the Standing Committee of the Henan Provincial Party Committee and secretary of the Zhengzhou Municipal Party Committee, visited Zhengzhou Airport Economy Zone for investigation and supervision many times. Xu proposed that Zhengzhou Airport Economy Zone should closely follow the functional layout of "Vibrating South Zhengzhou", adhere to planning guidance, strengthen overall coordination, plan and promote development and construction in an integrated way, and strive to build a highland for opening-up so as to play a role and provide support in accelerating the construction of National Central City and forming a high-quality development regional growth pole.

全力"的精神，以"爬坡过坎、滚石上山"的意志，以"披荆斩棘、勇毅笃行"的信念，经历了筚路蓝缕的求索，创出了沧海桑田的巨变。中国的航空大都市已傲然崛起，并在新的起点上瞄准了更高目标。它正张开有力的双翼，飞向充满无限可能的未来。

In November, 2020, Zhengzhou Airport Economy Zone held a meeting of leading cadres in the whole region, announcing the decision of the Provincial Party Committee on the adjustment of the main leaders of the Party Working Committee and the Management Committee of the Zhengzhou Airport Economy Zone. Zhang Junfeng holds the post of secretary of Party Working Committee of Zhengzhou Airport Economy Zone (Zhengzhou Xinzheng Comprehensive Bonded Zone), and Wan Zhengfeng holds the post of vice secretary of Party Working Committee of Zhengzhou Airport Economy Zone (Zhengzhou Xinzheng Comprehensive Bonded Zone) and director of Management Committee of the Zhengzhou Airport Economy Zone. Taking over the position is also taking over the blueprint of the Zhengzhou Airport Economy Zone. A magnificent picture of "a big transportation hub, an open gateway and an aviation metropolis" has been slowly unfolded, and the beautiful vision for the future is being turned into down-to-earth practice.

The Kunpeng roc spreads its wings and flies high into the sky. The Zhengzhou Airport Economy Zone, like the Kunpeng roc, is soaring up. With the spirit of "racing against time and exerting one's energy", the will of "climbing over the ridge and rolling stones up the mountain", and the belief of "overcoming difficulties and bravely walking", the Zhengzhou Airport Economy Zone has explored and finally created great changes. China's Aerotropolis is proudly rising and aiming at higher goals at a new starting point. The Zhengzhou Airport Economy Zone is spreading its powerful wings and flying to the future full of infinite possibilities.